GET OUT GET FREE

HOW TO ESCAPE A TOXIC OR ABUSIVE RELATIONSHIP *in Australia*

GET OUT GET FREE

HOW TO ESCAPE A TOXIC OR ABUSIVE RELATIONSHIP *in Australia*

By

LIZ ATHERTON

CONSCIOUS CARE PUBLISHING PTY LTD

GET OUT GET FREE
How to escape a toxic or abusive relationship in Australia

Copyright © 2018 by Liz Atherton. All rights reserved.

First Published 2018 by: Conscious Care Publishing Pty Ltd
www.consciouscarepublishing.com

First Edition printed October 2018.

Notice of Rights

This book is sold subject to the condition that it shall not, by way of trade or otherwise, be lent, resold, hired out, or otherwise circulated without the publisher's prior consent, in any form of binding or cover, other than that in which it is published, and without a similar condition, including this condition being imposed on the subsequent purchaser. All rights reserved by the publisher. No part of this publication may be reproduced, stored in a retrieval system, or transmitted in any form, or by any means, electronic, digital, mechanical, photocopying, scanning, recorded or otherwise, without the prior written permission of the copyright owner. Requests to the copyright owner should be addressed to Permissions Department, Conscious Care Publishing Pty Ltd, email: admin@consciouscare.com

Limits of Liability/Disclaimer of Warranty:

While the publisher and author have used their best efforts in preparing this book, they make no representations or warranties with respect to the accuracy or completeness of the contents of this book and specifically disclaim any implied warranties of merchantability or fitness for a particular purpose. No warranty may be created or extended by sales representatives or written sales materials. The advice and strategies contained herein may not be suitable for your situation. You should consult with a professional where appropriate. The intent of the author is only to offer information for a general nature. Neither the publisher nor author shall be liable for any loss of profit or any other commercial damages, including but not limited to special, incidental, consequential, or other damages. The author and the publisher assume no responsibility for your actions.

Where photographic images have been provided by the author and people are depicted, such images are being used for illustrative purposes only. Product names may be trademarks or registered trademarks, and are used for identification and explanation without intent to infringe. Conscious Care Publishing publishes in a variety of print and electronic format and by print-on-demand. Some material included with standard print versions of this book may not be included in e-books or in print-on-demand. If this book refers to media such as a CD or DVD that is not included in the version you purchased, you may download this material at www.getoutgetfree.com

National Library of Australia Cataloguing-in-Publication entry:

Author: Atherton, Liz 1963-

Get Out Get Free / by Liz Atherton

ISBN 9780648085492 (Paperback), 9780987633705 (Digital), 9780987633712 (Auditory)

Rocky Hudson, Editor.

Melissa Williams (LLB), Contributor.
Printed by Lightning Source

Typeset & cover design by Conscious Care Publishing Pty Ltd

362.8292

ISBN: 97978-0-6480854-9-2

Dedication

To you my reader, of any creed, colour, race or gender. May this book bring you love, hope and happiness in your life and relationships.

Comes the Dawn

After a while you learn the subtle difference
Between holding a hand and chaining a soul
And you learn that love doesn't mean leaning
And that company doesn't mean security
And presents aren't promised,
And you begin to accept your defeats
With your head up and your eyes open
With the grace of a woman, not the grief of a child.

And you learn to build all your roads
On today because tomorrow's ground
Is too uncertain for plans, and futures have
A way of falling down in mid-flight.

After a while you learn that even sunshine
Burns if you get too much
So you plant your own gardens and decorate
Your own soul, instead of waiting
For someone to bring you flowers.
And you learn that you really can endure…
That you really are strong
And you really do have worth

And you learn and learn with every goodbye
You learn….

Anon

Family & Domestic Violence....
"is an overt or subtle expression of power or imbalance, resulting in one person living in fear of another and usually involves an ongoing pattern of abuse characterised by coercive and controlling behaviours."

(National Risk Assessment Principles for domestic and family violence: Companion resource. A summary of the evidence-base supporting the development and implementation of the National Risk Assessment Principles for domestic and family violence / Corina Backhouse and Cherie Toivonen. Sydney, NSW: ANROWS, c2018.)

Contents

From the author	I
Acknowledgements	V
Introduction	1
Chapter 1: What is a healthy relationship?	**5**
Qualities to look for in a healthy relationship	5
Stages of a relationship	8
The triangular theory of love	14
Kinds of love	17
Your rights in or out of a relationship	20
Relationship myths	21
Is there uncertainty in your relationship?	27
Chapter 2: What is an unhealthy relationship?	**29**
Qualities to watch out for in an unhealthy relationship	30
Chapter 3: Is my relationship toxic or abusive?	**37**
Stress is a natural response	40

How do I feel today?	40
Stress symptoms	43
Anger as a signal	46
Attitudes and behaviours of people who use violence	48
High risk triggers	52
Am I in an abusive relationship?	53
Mental health issues	57
Your core beliefs	59
Chapter 4: FDV & its impact	**61**
The barriers of escaping FDV in a relationship	66
Defining trauma	70
Mental illness - signs and signals	71
Children of FDV	72
When to report children experiencing FDV	76
Stockholm syndrome	79
Chapter 5: The cycle of violence	**80**
Phase 1 - Build up and stand over	82
Phase 2 - Acute Violence or Explosion	84
Phase 3 - Honeymoon	85
Awareness of the cycle	87
Unconscious need for love	88
Cultural barriers	92
Chapter 6 - Stopping the cycle of violence	**97**
Your happiness counts	98
Ego -vs- Self	101

Hurt people, hurt people	104
High risk indicators	106
Support network	107
Safety planning	109
Solutions to consequences of staying or leaving	113
Working through fears to exit your relationship	117
Escalation of the violence	118
Increased chances of being killed	120
Damage to property	124
Children may be targeted or hurt protecting me	125
Increased risk of abuse during contact	125
Can't stop abuser regardless of restraining order	128
Might have to move out of family home	129
Living on less money as a single parent	131
Child support may be slow arriving or avoid paying	133
Unable to make loan repayments/credit destroyed	134
Might have to quit job to take care of children	135
Might threaten your employment	136
Destroy things of importance	137
Might have to go into hiding, move, leave town	137
You do not have enough income to go to court	138
No access to phone or technology	140
May continue abuse through access	141
Might use drugs or alcohol to cope	142
Have family and friends threatened	143

Might not have the support from family or friends	144
Suicidal thoughts or commit suicide	145
May have language difficulties	147
May have cultural challenges with support	147
Might be deported or children taken	148
Dishonour to my family or culture	148
Support	148
Rebuilding you	150
Chapter 7: Your legal rights	**153**
Should I get a restraining order?	157
Parental Alienation	161
Attending Local Court	162
Evidence for Local Court	163
Evidence for Family Court	164
Family Court Mediation	165
Legal Representation	167
Your application for parenting orders	168
Breach of parenting orders	177
Orders against a child's will	181
Chapter 8: Moving Forward	**188**
Choosing your partners carefully	190
References	194
Further Information	196

From the Author

With life now well adjusted and moving forward I am inspired to write a book to assist others on their journey to healing and happiness following toxic or abusive relationships. Many years have passed for me to be able to achieve my personal freedom from abuse that has stemmed back as far as my childhood and was part of my adult relationships. Attempting to learn boundaries and using them wasn't an easy feat, but has been most rewarding. If only I had the help and insight that I am offering you; the advice to stand tall and say no to abuse would have made my journey much easier. I write this book to spread my loving support to others to help them identify and acknowledge abuse and how to disentangle themselves from abusive relationships, or just relationships that are not loving and supportive to them as a human being and do not honour their individuality.

Abuse can be delivered in many forms. You may not even be able to articulate what you are going through. Within these pages I write about these many different forms of abuse, and explain how subtle emotional, physical, financial, sexual and legal abuse can be. It wasn't until I reached out and attended a domestic violence community group meeting, that I could even establish what I was experiencing in an adult relationship. I had mistakenly believed domestic violence could only be physical.

Life is too short to be unhappy. I have seen my darling Mother go through very similar situations to what I have endured, God Bless her – guilt and worry meant she never had the strength to leave these situations. My Mother passed over with a heavy weight on her heart: she had loved her children very deeply but had somehow felt she had failed to protect us.

I have moved through many emotions, including hurt, deep sadness, anger, rage and love; I learned self-protection, self-love and then forgiveness throughout my healing over the years. I have experienced heartfelt love and support from the universe, my friends and family during the deepest darkest hours of my journey. My love for my children and the want for an abuse-free life has motivated me in the toughest of times. I was once a care taker, putting many others first before myself, giving everything of myself away to seek love and approval. Now I am a strong, grounded woman who takes care of herself first and others second.

In today's society there is much shame in suffering from abuse, and exposing abusers carries tremendous risk. Should you expose the family or relationship secrets that have laid dormant for months or years, secrets which perpetrators masterfully attempt to hide in the walls of their homes, you are likely to feel outcast from the family and often society. This imposed emotional imprisonment is extremely difficult to break free from, and the first step to take is to acknowledge the imprisonment. Many are not prepared to take this step because of how alone they feel on their journey. Everyone suffering this type persecution can ask themselves the question: I am truly deeply happy? Inherently we know the deep answer even if we are not ready to hear or face it. When one shares their experience, it opens the door to acknowledgement and many mixed emotions. What is acknowledged cannot be ignored, even if no action is taken.

I wish to share with you not just my journey but those of many men and women who have walked my road and shared their life experiences too. I have talked and shared my experiences with many without feeling guilt or shame, but it didn't start out that way.

May the information and guidance within this book take the heaviness from your heart and soul to bring you peace and joy. As I hold your hand, know too that I have travelled the path of fear, struggle, disbelief and danger. You have the right as a human to be safe and live the life you were born to live, regardless of your purpose in this world.

You can't let the sorrow from the past destroy your future. Today is yours. Your choice. Your freedom. Your happiness. Grab it with both hands. Seek the life you dream of. You and your children are worth it, as am I.

With strength and love, achieve new heights.

Acknowledgements

How can I thank an abuser you might ask?

How do we see the persecution that we may have experienced as bringing about self-growth? Without my experiences, I couldn't help you, and I truly believe that is my purpose.

I have always been a natural supporter, educator and trainer. I even have a "School Counsellor" badge from year 9 of high school. People are my thing. I love to help open the minds of others to their greater inner wealth and joy. I love to see them shining their own beacons of light, rather than being led around like sheep in the world, trying to fit into everyone else's shadows. We are all born innately individual. However, school, governments, families and cultures treat us the same, educating us to fit a mould that isn't perfect for each individual.

Firstly, I would like to thank my dear father, who suffered from brain damage prior to my birth, and my darling mother who nursed his return to health and did her absolute best for us all.

My father just wasn't the same man after his accident and my mother's love for him made her stay until the safety of a sibling was in jeopardy. Watching his alcoholism and my mum suffer financially in my young teens was a journey.

My mother was an angel on earth who had the capacity to love everyone, both good and bad, regardless of their colour, race or experience. Unfortunately, stress took a toll on her body and she left us at the young age of 63. My mum is still my guiding light of love as I hold her ability within me to love under the toughest of conditions. I loved and fought for my own and my children's freedom from an abuser. Then I chose to no longer suffer in the same ways my mum did. I chose to fight back, to fight against the powers of my abuser, the court system and anything else in my way.

The fight was exhausting but certainly worth every second of my time. I didn't realise what I had got caught up in until I saw how those with money can manipulate others. My abuser used his money and my lack of knowledge to fight me through the courts, claiming that I was the abuser and was alienating him from his child.

I had support throughout the journey from an extremely fantastic psychologist, Karen Michael in Sydney, Australia. Without her I truly would've have made it! Thank you, Karen from the bottom of my heart for your professional accolades, kindness and willingness to propel me and my family away from suffering abuse.

Without my experience of abuse from my family of origin, including siblings, I couldn't have stood tall. Without watching my mother suffer emotionally, financially and physically I wouldn't have acknowledged the way I chose to be free of that in my adulthood. Yet with the conditioning of abuse I experienced, it had somehow become the way I expected a relationship to be; rather than walk away, I would fight for my rights to be respected and happy. My conditioning meant I managed to find numerous partners who didn't respect my needs, but truly I kept trying to fix them to feel love. What I didn't realise was that the partners were that way inclined and I couldn't change another being. They didn't have the capacity to love me respectfully. I had many hard lessons, in particular a major relationship with a partner who was destructively controlling. I thank him for the experience – I can help you now because of that. I truly feel sorry for his feelings of fear of loss, and the need for love and security, which drove him to control his environment so intensely.

My journey has been difficult to say the least, but my journey shall lighten yours, and despite of it, I have had many people love and support me in return. To my best and oldest friends Kerry & John Ramsay, you both inspire me with your steadfast ways.

Melissa Williams (LLB), you continue to guide me to bring the most up-to-date information on Family Law. May we travel this path together fueling our passion and purpose to help, guide and inspire others to set boundaries as safely as possible and live the happy life they deserve. Your inspiration is likened to mine, with determination, grit and love all bundled together. Let's make a difference to enlighten and invoke change in a positive way to those lost through lack of knowledge, power or money!

To my darling children Katie and Lachlan, for whom I gave every cell in my body to keep fighting. You are the truest loves of my life. Now and eternally.

Katie, you have come through to help me learn boundaries with men. From a very young age, you knew who you were. You assert yourself beautifully and own everything that you are. Thank you for your loving support when times were tough and I couldn't always be there for you. You have been the best 'girlfriend' I could have asked for. You helped make me strong and resilient having you by my side, especially after losing my mum.

Lachlan, you were the first man that truly loved me, warts and all. You were my inspiration to find a partner who could love me with the love, dedication and protection you have shown me. You are an inspiration, with your strong spirit for justice, devoted to those that stand beside you, strong yet soft enough, and the determination to be better than your role model. You'll make a fabulous father and partner because of your lessons.

Introduction

Enough is enough! There is so much normalised violence in Australia and the rest of the world. There are strong social norms permitting violence: we watch and experience violence regularly in our own homes, local streets and city social locations. This norm of social acceptance of violence filters into our subconscious, acclimatising us to see violence as normal, especially if it has been within our own homes, inflicted by our family members or through the media we watch. Even exposure to negative news, via the TV, radio or internet, can normalise violent behaviour. With alcohol and drugs so prevalent in the world, these too have affects on behaviours, often triggering violence that may be tolerated by victims. The mental health of our loved ones is also an important factor in determining how much abuse we will tolerate when trying to assist them to recover.

What exactly is violence and at what level should you decide it can't be tolerated? Everyone's experience of aggression and abuse is extremely varied, depending on their prior exposure to different levels of anger, their coping methods and also the depth or regularity of exposure to abuse.

This book was written to help you establish if you are suffering from an abusive or toxic relationship, to teach you how to safely establish boundaries, even if you have left your relationship and to give guidance on exiting an abusive relationship and how to meander through the legal systems. It encompasses the legal paths you can choose should you not be able to communicate and set the expected levels of respect from your loved ones, including those who are passive aggressive. You will also learn, step-by-step, how to protect and preserve yourself during the most stressful times. Through reading this book you will be able to establish whether a relationship you have – whether with a partner, child, parent, sibling or member of your extended family – is destructive to your wellbeing, and if the love you have for someone is being used to manipulate or control you, directly or via your children.

You should not have to tolerate abuse. However, there are many people struggling with their own issues and demons who affect all those around them, the people closest to them as well as strangers. But how do you know what you should tolerate, and what are the indicators that show you that you are suffering either mentally, physically or emotionally?

Within these pages are detailed descriptions of both physical and psychological warning signs of *Family & Domestic Violence ("FDV")*. I'll teach you how to plan your safe exit as a *Victim* (a person subjected to FDV) through the legal system in Australia and establish firm boundaries with the *Perpetrator* or *Abuser* (a person who chooses to use violence). Australia's laws are differ-

INTRODUCTION

ent within each state, and you need to know what applies to your state and how to go about enforcing safe and legal boundaries to protect you from the people who use violence against you.

I write from both my own experiences and those of others. Australian communities are slowly recognising the devastating impact FDV has on the victims and their children. FDV is closeted in disgust within the community, even though the statistics are so dramatically high. Victims of abuse, even at a psychological level, can be devastated without proper support and guidance. Slowly but surely the victims of FDV will be more supported in Australia. Only recently has the Australian Government introduced leave for FDV victims. However, corporations and small business often do not have strategies in place to protect and support their employees, and even local governments are only just starting to implement policies and practices for FDV leave.

This book is to give you the knowledge on setting boundaries, even if you have left your relationship, to help prevent you from suffering to the degree that both I and many others have suffered, and it is written to help prevent the devastating effect of FDV on your life and the lives of your children, especially when having to face the legal systems and obstacles.

The information contained within is a guidance for you, and you may require further legal assistance on the process of safely exiting an abusive relationship. This book is to help collaborate the many avenues you may need to explore to seek support and get free from abuse, depending on your personal choices and the options available.

Your journey may appear daunting and freeing yourself from abusers and those enabling abuse can be like getting an octopus off you one leg at a time whilst the other seven are actively re-attaching themselves. But I will show you the light at the end of the tunnel. The strategies and methods within this book should help you on your travels. It should provide an overal perspective of the opportunities and obstacles you may have to face in getting the freedom you deserve.

Accepting that your relationship with a loved one is abusive is your first step towards healing. Loving yourself (and your children) more than your abuser is the second. The third is to choose a safe and happy life. The fourth is to move forward towards that life, one day at a time.

Once you acknowledge the effects of FDV, this book shall give you the guidance to find resources and move forward. It will empower you to live a safe and happy life. I truly hope this book changes your path.

What is a healthy relationship?

A healthy relationship is one that is based on healthy communication and behaviours. This means being able to effectively communicate your needs and wants. Both parties should exhibit non-threatening behaviours which allow the respective partners to speak and act in a way that makes the other feel safe to be themselves. Every relationship has some difficulties and conflict, but this can be managed within a healthy relationship. Dealing with problems through open and truthful communication is one of the features that defines a healthy relationship.

The need for trust and support is paramount. Within a healthy relationship there is a fundamental need for honesty, responsibility, accountability, and acknowledgment of misdemeanours that affect your partner.

Qualities to look for in a healthy relationship

A healthy relationship should be based on friendship, love, equality, fairness, trust, honesty and mutual respect. Not every man or woman will have all these qualities, but they should be willing to work on those which they lack, particularly in these areas:

Open and effective communication

- Sharing of ideas and opinions
- Making your partner feel sufficiently safe and supported to share
- Allowing the other to feel heard
- Providing a comfortable space to openly share how you feel
- Willingness to talk through problems
- Sharing your expectations of the relationship
- Being non-judgemental
- Working towards satisfying resolutions to conflict

Feelings of safety

- Peacefulness
- Security
- Happiness
- Dignity
- The absence of addiction issues such as alcohol, drugs, work, sex and gambling

Sharing

- Shared values
- Common tasks and interests
- Sense of humour
- The ability to have fun

WHAT IS A HEALTHY RELATIONSHIP

Commitment

- Be prepared to maintain the positive aspects of the relationship and work on any issue as it may arise
- Provide trust and support
- Empower each other
- Taking responsibility for your own actions and happiness
- Giving yourself freely and unconditionally

Equality

- Shared commitment to an equal relationship
- Mutual decisions and agreements
- Equal power / no abuse of power
- Respecting the values of your partner

Differences and individuality

- Being free to be yourself
- Maintaining a sense of self and an ability to provide for your own needs
- Accepting and respecting each other's choice of friends and activities
- Accepting and celebrating the differences in each other
- Having separate identities
- Building self-esteem and confidence
- Respecting each other's rights as an individual
- Accepting the other's goals
- Respecting each other's space

Growth
- Personal growth - Relationship growth - Encouragement of each other
Intimacy
- Emotional - the sharing of feelings - Acceptance of spiritual beliefs - Physical intimacy, with or without sex, including spontaneity, romance and affection in front of others

A relationship is a container of energy that sits between two people. It is a place to love and respect each other and to provide commitment to the needs of the relationship. This sacred space between two people should be managed with a mutual contribution to the nurturing of the relationship, with both parties agreeing to contribute to certain aspects of the relationship so that it remains healthy. Therefore, a relationship requires nurturing to grow and strengthen. With neglect it can weaken and decline. Investment of time, energy and commitment is essential for its continuation.

Stages of a relationship

Relationships move through different stages and growth periods. Some couples develop a well-balanced relationship extremely quickly, and for others it can be a lifelong process and never end, depending on the commitment of each individual to the relation-

WHAT IS A HEALTHY RELATIONSHIP

ship and their life experiences and circumstances.

Healthy relationships are a great way to learn about yourself. Through listening to your partner, reflecting on the truth and your contribution to the problems within the relationship, and taking responsibility for your contribution to the good, bad and ugly of your relationship you develop self-awareness. Both parties must take the relationship seriously and nurture the other whilst taking responsibility for their contribution to it.

Communication theorist Mark Knapp, in his 1984 book Interpersonal *Communications and Human Relationships*[1], broke the rise and fall of relationships into ten steps, as detailed in the table on the next pages. You may find you go through these stages of a relationship and also move forwards and backwards through various steps:

GET OUT GET FREE

Process	Stage	Representative Dialogue
Coming Together	Initiating	"Hi, how you doing?" "Fine. You?" Initiating contact to show that you are interested in making contact with someone and you are worth talking to. It is normally brief and may seem superficial and may involve talking about the weather or friendly expression.
	Experimenting	"Oh, so you like to ski…so do I." "You do? Great. Where do you go?" Experimenting is trying to find common ground and is still small talk and helps us decide whether the person is worth pursuing and a safe way to ease into a relationship. The quality of the communication changes after a small amount of this stage and may move into disclosing more personal information which increases the attraction to one another.
	Intensifying	"I…I think I love you." "I love you too." This stage is where couples try to be more attractive to each other, discuss the state of the relationship and their feelings of attraction, spend increasing time together, asking for …cont'd…

WHAT IS A HEALTHY RELATIONSHIP

Process	Stage	Representative Dialogue
	Intensifying cont'd	support from one another, doing favours, affection, hinting, flirting and non-verbal expression of feelings, meeting friends and family. Even though commitment intensifies, doubts still remain and use strategies to test the partner that prove their level of commitment.
Coming Together cont'd	Integrating	"I feel so much a part of you." "Yeah, we are like one person. What happens to you happens to me." Integration is where the relationship strengthens and become a social unit and are acknowledged as a couple. The "I" becomes a "We" and sense of obligation to the other grows. Requests are generally straightforward, and they expect more from one another than they do in less intimate stages.
	Bonding	"I want to be with you always." "Let's get married." A new stage to show the world that your "We" exists and marks a turning point to one of commitment and a critical period where outsiders acknowledge the relationship and can take the form of a licence to be married and generates social support for the relationship.

GET OUT GET FREE

Process	Stage	Representative Dialogue
Coming Apart	Differentiating	"I just don't like big social gatherings." "Sometimes I don't understand you. This is one area where I'm certainly not like you at all." After formally commonality in bonding they need to reestablish individuality which can move from "We" to "I" but can be positive for individuals and parts of a relationship.
	Circumscribing	"Did you have a good time on your trip?" "What time will dinner be ready?" This can be a plateau development stage and can last a lifetime, however some relationships decline and dissolve. Communication can often decrease in quality and quantity together with subtle dissatisfaction hints and behaviours such as less romance, more arguments and working later. Rather than sorting through disagreements, partners can withdraw or physical withdraw without total avoidance but more shrinking of interest and involvement.
	Stagnating	"What's there to talk about?" "Right. I know what you are going to say and you know what I am going to say." ...cont'd...

WHAT IS A HEALTHY RELATIONSHIP

Process	Stage	Representative Dialogue
	Stagnating cont'd	If circumscribing continues the relationship shall stagnate and no growth happens which becomes a hollow shell with loss of enthusiasm with no sense of joy with repeated events.
	Avoiding	"I'm so busy. I just don't know when I will be able to see you." "If I'm not around when you try, you'll understand." This stage partners will create distance avoid the relationship by using excuses and be very direct about their needs and is often the indicator that the relationship is dead.
Coming Apart	Terminating	"I'm leaving you…and don't bother trying to contact me." "Don't worry, I won't." This stage one or both partners will terminate the relationship with a cordial dinner, a note, text message, phone call or legal document. This process may be short or drawn out with bitter jabs at each other, depending on whether the parties are in agreement of the termination. If one partner ends the relationship and the other doesn't want to, communication can become harsh.

The triangular theory of love

What does it mean to love someone? Loving someone can take varied forms and experiences. Love is a complex psychological emotion that is influenced by many things, such as your genetically transmitted instincts and drives and also socially learned role modelling from your parents or guardians and even your culture.

Love has many aspects and can be experienced differently in many relationships. According to renowned psychologist Robert J. Sternberg's theory of interpersonal relationships, love has three components. The theory is that each of the components lie within the heart of most human relationships. Sternberg's theory is that these three components form the vertices of a triangle and each of these components can be used in many different ways to form seven different love types.

Within Sternberg's theory there are three different components: (a) *intimacy*, which encompasses the feelings of closeness, connectedness, and bonds one experiences in loving relationships; (b) *passion*, which encompasses the drives that lead to romance, physical attraction, and sexual consummation; and (c) *decision/commitment*, which encompasses, in the short term, the decision that one loves another, and in the long term, the commitment to maintain that love. The amount of love one experiences depends on the absolute strength of these three components, and the kind of love one experiences depends on their strengths relative to each other. The three components interact with each other and with the actions that they produce and that produce them so as to form a number of different kinds of loving experiences.[2]

WHAT IS A HEALTHY RELATIONSHIP

In general, the *intimacy* component might be viewed as largely, but not exclusively, deriving from emotional investment in the relationship; the *passion* component as deriving largely, although not exclusively, from motivational involvement in the relationship; and the *decision/commitment* component as deriving largely, although not exclusively, from cognitive decision in and commitment to the relationship. From one point of view, the *intimacy* component might be viewed as a "warm" one, the *passion* component as a "hot" one, and the *decision/commitment* component as a "cold" one.[2]

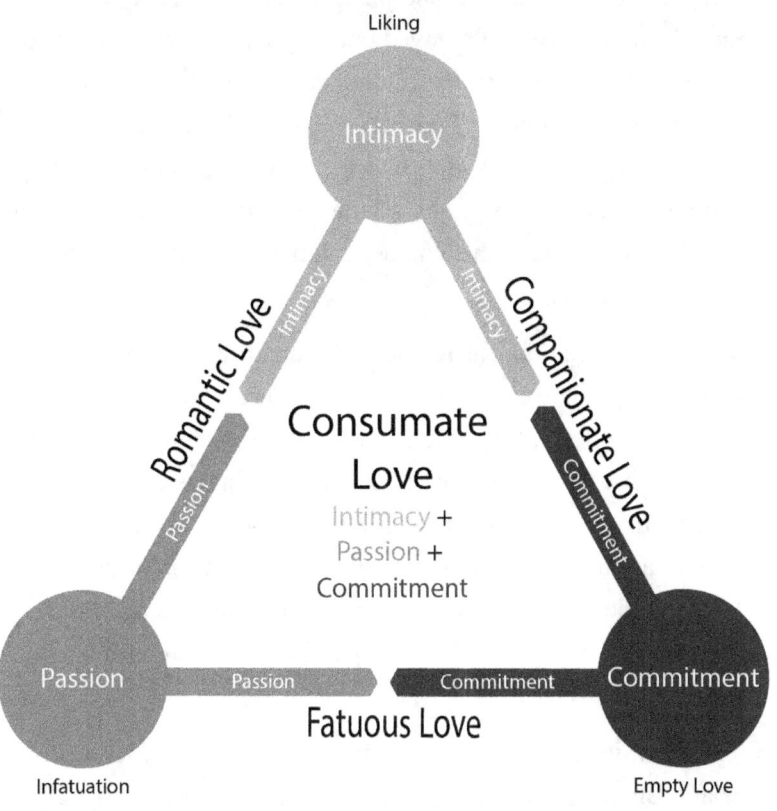

These three main components are not the only partitions of love. A combination of these components form seven different love types, but is important not to lose the importance of each component.

The *intimacy* component of love is at the core of many loving relationships, not only between lovers, but also between siblings, close friends, and parents and children. This intimacy component will often drive you to promote others' welfare, experience happiness with them and hold them in high regard. Intimacy allows mutual understanding, sharing of one another, being able to receive and give support, and being able to intimately communicate with and value the loved one in your life. You do not require all of these aspects to feel intimacy within the relationship, but a sufficient number of feelings will establish this component. Consider the different ways you love your father/mother, sibling and best friend, or lover. Not all the feelings you have for these people will be within this component, but you still feel intimacy with each person.

The *passion* component tends to be found mostly in romantic relationships, however you may experience low levels of this component, if at all, in love for a parent, especially a same-sex parent. This passion component creates an intense longing for sexual fulfilment or union with another, but is not required in filial relationships, such as a relationship with a son or daughter. Psychological arousal may create physiological arousal, with one kind leading to another. However passion can be aroused by intimacy or vice versa.

The commitment component can be variable within different love relationships. It is a major part of your intense love of your children but may not be significant in your relationships with friends that come and go throughout your life. This component has two parts, a short-term one where one decides to love another, and long-term decision to maintain the love. It is important in loving relationships not to ignore the commitment if it does not have the "heat" of passion and intimacy. This component is what keeps a relationship going with its ups and downs.

In summary of these three components, they are all important parts of a loving relationship even though their importance differs from one relationship to another and over time.

Kinds of Love

Considering the different components, the mixture of these three different components make up seven kinds of love and one of non-love.

1. **Non-love**. Non-love is simply the absence of all three components of love. This is the large majority of casual interactions without love.

2. **Liking**. This is where you may experience only friendship but feel a closeness, warmth or bond towards another without feeling passionate or wanting a long-term commitment.

3. **Infatuated love**. This is "love at first sight" feelings of passionate arousal without intimacy or commitment. The heart beating or palpitations, adrenaline rush, hormonal rush or the instant psycho-physiological "turn-on". This type of love can dissipate as quickly as it rises, or it can last the distance under the right circumstances.

4. **Empty love**. This kind of love is devoid of intimacy and passion components and people often find themselves in stagnant or distanced relationships where they have lost the emotional involvement and physical attraction. This can often be the stage of love before the relationship ends.

5. **Romantic love**. A combination of intimacy and passionate components, where attraction is drawn by physical aspects but the pair are bonded emotionally. This view is often found in literature and movies of "undying intense love".

6. **Companionate love**. A combination of intimacy and commitment components. This type of love often takes the form of a long-term committed friendship, such as a marriage where physical attraction has died down.

7. **Fatuous love**. A combination of passion and commitment components, lacking the intimacy. This is often the whirlwind romance type of love that leads to couples marrying quickly. Because the commitment is made on the basis of passion without real intimacy, divorce may result when the intimacy is not developed.

8. **Consummate love**. A combination of all three components, where complete love results. It is the kind of love we all strive for in romantic relationships. This is the ultimate goal in relationships with partners, and isn't necessarily difficult to obtain or maintain, nor is there any guarantee it will last.

WHAT IS A HEALTHY RELATIONSHIP

Taxonomy of Kinds of Love Table[3]

Kind of Love	Component		
	Intimacy	Passion	Commitment
Non Love			
Liking	✓		
Infatuated Love		✓	
Empty Love			✓
Romantic Love	✓	✓	
Companionate Love	✓		✓
Fatuous Love		✓	✓
Consummate Love	✓	✓	✓

Note. ✓ = component present; blank = component absent. These kinds of love represent limiting cases based on the triangular theory. Most loving relationships will fit between categories, because the various components of love are expressed along continua, not discretely.

The table above may help you establish the type of loving relationship you may be in, or may open a discussion with your partner to seek and sustain the type of love you want to develop. It will also help you ascertain what is offered to you from a prospective partner if you are looking for love, or trying to avoid being trapped in a relationship that isn't fulfilling your 'love' needs.

Your rights in or out of a relationship

Remember under no circumstances should you give up your rights within a relationship. If you are giving these up you probably need to ask yourself why. Are you making the decision to give up your rights for the sake of maintaining the relationship and sacrificing your happiness in the process? Balancing the needs of both parties will contribute to a healthy relationship, but if you give up your rights, you give up your happiness.

You and others have these rights at all times in your life:

- A right to your own values and needs
- A right to express how you feel, including negative emotions
- A right to offer no excuses for your behaviour
- A right to make mistakes, take responsibility and suffer consequences for them
- A right to change your mind when you see fit
- A right to make your own decisions, regardless of the needs of anyone else
- A right to say that you don't know, you don't care or you don't understand, at anytime you need to
- A right to make yourself feel good and to praise yourself regardless of the opinion of others
- A right to say no at anytime to anyone without feeling guilty or selfish
- A right to spend your time how you see fit and in ways that you choose

- A right to ask for affection, help, time or information from others
- A right to refuse to provide affection, help, time or information.

Often, we assume our partner will contribute to the relationship in ways we expect based on our own prior experiences from our family of origin and culture, as well as from prior relationships. When you have unspoken expectations of what your relationship should be and fail to communicate these to your partner, this is often the cause of distress within the relationship. Where one party has an expectation of how they should be treated and has failed to communicate or be heard, the other party is unaware of their expectations. As a result, conflict may occur, and it is imperative you have a safe place to share how you feel and enough investment from the other party to recreate new agreements for the health and longevity of the relationship. This type of open communication is what makes a relationship survive.

Learning to communicate in a healthy manner can be hard. You may struggle to openly ask for your needs in a way that your partner can hear you. Do you struggle to find the words to articulate what you need, or are you too scared to ask because you fear losing your relationship? If so, you are gunny sacking (a fight tactic to save up grievances), giving yourself up for the sake of the relationship. It is when you are in this position you may be in an unhealthy relationship.

Relationship myths

Love can change over time. As explained in the different love types, a relationship can grow or dissipate in a short or long period of time, depending on the wants, needs and effort of both partners.

Are you influenced by idealistic information about loving relationships, such as those depicted in novels, songs and on television? From childhood we begin to absorb information about love and relationships and how they are supposed to be. Children see how our parents relate to one another, and receive sex education at school and amongst their peers, but none of us are educated on what is and what isn't a healthy relationship. We all romanticise love, thinking that love will last. People grow and change and even the *consummate* love relationships may not last.

As we grow individually, so do our needs. Being able to adapt to the changing needs of one another requires that you be committed to one another's happiness. It is necessary to embrace the needs of the other for growth and grow together. Relationships do get close and then move apart. This is a natural progression as you tackle your individuality within the relationship and then seek the bond of love at the same time.

Unfortunately and innately, women tend to romanticise love. They all want the *romantic* love, their hero knight in shining armour to sweep them up and fling them on the back of a white horse and ride off into the distance. Men, however, see this as a romantic way of capturing a women's heart; it does not mean they want to spend a lifetime rescuing their damsels in distress.

We all need to learn to be an individual in a relationship, where we don't give up any parts of ourselves and bring our entire being into the relationship. Relationships all end, either by separation or death. At some stage you will be an individual on your own

WHAT IS A HEALTHY RELATIONSHIP

again so it is important to never lose your individuality. It is a mistake to become dependent on your partner for everything, including your happiness.

Sometimes you may feel that you only like your partner, but doesn't mean you have fallen out of love. When passion starts to rescind, your love type may be changing. With the pressures of life – such as children, work and finances – you may begin to doubt your love for each other because of the lack of time for the commitment to the relationship and need for coupling. Take the time out to discuss your relationship needs and make time for the relationship so that everything else isn't always the priority.

Not all loving relationships last a lifetime. It is a myth that one special other can fulfil all your needs – intellectually, socially, emotionally, sexually – and be your only companion and the only one you spend social times with. Those who expect that from another person have a dire need for security. It is imperative to look at your own insecurities and ask yourself if you put too much pressure on one person to fulfil your needs. This pressure can lead to a partner feel trapped, smothered and resentful, and can kill the love between you.

If your partner feels love for someone else, then are they not capable of loving you more? People believe they have a certain amount of love to give, when the core of you (your soul) has bountiful amounts of love to give. The capacity to love is limitless. We have a number of relationships with parents, children, friends, siblings and partners. Love is not limited, and jealousy over your partner loving another is not natural, and is an expression of your insecurity and lack of confidence in yourself and your relationship. Being free to love many people is a natural disposition, and shows others that you have a natural expression of love. Having many loving relationships should make your partner feel more secure. Jealous behaviour will make you feel interrogated, stalked and accountable for every minute of your day, and will drive a relationship apart. A partner may have sexual attraction to another person but doesn't mean they are less attracted to you. Most partners choose not to act on those feelings when in a relationship and will exercise self-control. Having these feelings of attraction does not mean they are devaluing the relationship or you. Partners need to discuss intimacy outside of their relationship and agree on what works for them.

It is not true that you will always know how and what the other person is thinking and feeling. Living together for any length of time doesn't give you 'mind reading' ability. Don't assume that you know how your partner thinks and feels and stop listening or asking. You might guess or assume, but people change and grow. You may not know exactly what is going on for them, so ask and listen, don't assume by their non-verbal behaviour that you know everything. You might guess right but no-one likes to be told how they are thinking or feeling. You have to accept that what they say is what they mean. If their actions and words are not congruent, ask. Otherwise, expect an argument to arise if you assume and are wrong. Mind reading can be destructive as it doesn't clarify anything.

Love doesn't make good communication. Willingness to be open and vulnerable does. Some people believe they communicate well, but what on level are they communicating? Are you prepared to only talk about safe topics or surface issues within your relationship? Are you bottling up feelings or denying your partner's feelings or opinions? Are you being defensive, aggressive or passive aggressive in order to control the communication? Good communication requires speaking, listening, learning, practice and effort. There are three basics skills of good communication: 1) telling your partner how you feel; 2) listening (not mind reading); and 3) accepting your partner's opinions and feelings even if they are different from your own.

It is a common myth that when the relationship is in trouble, one partner is to blame. Every time you accuse your partner of having bad behaviours that damage your relationship, you label your partner as deficient in aspects of their compatibility to you. This doesn't resolve the issues in the relationship, it just highlights the differences. It is important to identify the differences of personal characteristics which may be causing distress in the relationship and review your own contribution to the problem rather than finger pointing. Every action has a re-action. Check out your reaction. If you continue to blame and not take responsibility for your contribution to the problem, the relationship cannot move forward and may end. Both partners must be willing to review the problem, their thinking and their behaviour for the continuation and success of the relationship.

Fighting in relationships only serves a destructive purpose and often does not clear the air for you to make up and feel good. Fighting is where you throw everything into the argument to win the war. Other things that you are not happy about should be dealt with as a separate issue, not stacked up to help you win the argument. Bringing in other issues is often referred to as gaslighting. Side-tracking – where more irrelevant issues are thrown in to distract from the problem being brought up – is another tactic used in fighting, as is bringing up previous misdeeds and mistakes. Being the one who only attends to what you want, where you don't want to address issues of the other and will dismiss their needs, is yet another tactic. Finally, there is character assassination, where you denigrate, criticise, over-exaggerate and say hurtful things in order to gain power.

When a problem arises in a relationship there has to be a win-win for both partners. It is a common myth that the argument can only end if one partner gives in or admits they are wrong (win-lose). This resolution to an argument is not a great way to resolve conflict, as sometimes arguments are over factual matters and you may need time to find out more facts. However, most arguments are not over factual matters, but rather stem from differences in opinions, feelings and experiences. Arguing to convince your partner your way is right and that they need to abandon their opinion, feelings and thoughts is destructive. Keeping the peace should not be dependent on one partner being submissive. Healthy relationships appreciate the differences and it is necessary to accept each partner's individuality and their right to think or feel differently. When differences in values and goals arise, the next step is to negotiate a resolution which suits both partners to gain the win-win.

Nagging is common but often doesn't give you the result you want. Nagging will not get your partner to do something they don't want to do by choice. Nagging isn't necessarily repetitive whinging and can take the form of sulking in silence or being a martyr in order to attempt to coerce your partner to do something they don't want to do. This indicates the relationship doesn't have open communication and lacks problem-solving skills.

WHAT IS A HEALTHY RELATIONSHIP

When both parties use different tactics to control each other's behaviours, communication and problem-solving only deteriorates.

Who said sex should be great when you love each other? Sex education at school stinks. You learn about the reproductive system and how to avoid becoming a parent. You are not educated on how to enjoy pleasurable sex, let alone how to have it in a relationship of some kind. We are all expected to learn about sex in relationships, but are not taught the fundamentals of the complicated skill of love and sex combined. In school and through our parents or peers we learn how to cook, clean, swim, play, work and drive. Love making doesn't always come naturally to everyone. It is a learned art and is different with each partner, as each person's needs and preferences are different, not to mention their sexual organs. Often masturbation is taboo within cultures, particularly for women, so often knowing how to be pleased can be a learning experience with a partner. Love doesn't automatically gift you with good sex. It grows from two people who are willing to have realistic expectations of each other, learning to be comfortable with their own sexual needs and expressing those needs through shared open communication and a willingness to enjoy the pleasure together.

Is there uncertainty in your relationship?

Every relationship has its ups and downs, conflict and uncertainty. Think about your relationship and some of the good things about the relationship. Think about how you have managed to work through the differences you've had with your partner. Asking yourself these questions and answering them honestly will give you a basis to start to work through some of the issues you need to address:

- Do we treat each other well?
- Are we loving toward each other and the relationship?
- Are we deeply caring, respectful and supportive to each other?
- Do we listen to each other without twisting issues and responsibilities?
- Can we share the difficult times we individually experience, including personal issues, dreams and hopes?
- Can we forgive each other?
- Do I feel safe emotionally, physically and financially?
- Are there certain aspects or issues of my life I feel I can't discuss?
- Do we accept each other as we are and avoid trying to change each other?
- Do we share fun and interesting activities together?
- Do we avoid criticising, judging or blaming each other?
- Can I be me in this relationship?
- Was the relationship fantastic in the beginning but now having issues you are not addressing?

In the next chapter we will be covering aspects of an unhealthy relationship and what behaviours and feelings you may be experiencing.

What is an unhealthy relationship

An unhealthy relationship is one that is based on unhealthy communication and behaviours. This means being unable to effectively communicate your needs and wants. An unhealthy relationship would exhibit some threatening behaviours, where your partner speaks or acts in a way that makes you feel unsafe and unable to be yourself. These behaviours could be of an emotional, financial, sexual, physical, social and/or spiritual nature. In Chapter 1, we discussed how every relationship has some difficulties and conflict, but how it is managed is what makes it a healthy relationship.

Discerning if your relationship is unhealthy will give you an avenue to attempt to sort through the issues and acknowledge the problem areas. However, not all partners are willing to sort through issues, and you may need to establish if the relationship is worthy of more input from you. In this chapter I will help you establish where things are not balanced in your relationship, and where to start giving yourself permission to be happy.

It can be very confusing for your relationship status or love type when the goals of the relationship are changing regularly for one or both partners. When people avoid being confronted about their lack of commitment and fail to follow through on agreed obligations, then arguments can follow. In a healthy relationship, arguments will be managed well to ensure a win-win for both partners.

Keep in mind that in a healthy relationship there is a fundamental need for trust, support, honesty, responsibility, accountability, and acknowledgment of misdemeanours that affect your partner.

An unhealthy relationship may on the surface appear to be healthy. However, the partners possibly have different needs and expectations, and this can cause conflict. It is important to establish what you both expect from a relationship early on, and define what your own personal long term needs and goals are for the type of relationship you want to be in.

We often get into a relationship without discussing our own personal wants and needs, out of fear that the other person, who we would like to begin with, will leave. When doing this, we give up our needs to gain the relationship, and thus are already suppressing ourselves. We must learn to put our needs and wants first, then see if the relationship fits those needs. Not the other way around.

Qualities to watch out for in an unhealthy relationship

An unhealthy relationship may be with a partner who is unwilling to work towards improving the relationship, has different

WHAT IS AN UNHEALTHY RELATIONSHIP

goals and needs, and generally doesn't really know what they want at the outset.

Often people enter relationships because of a sense of loneliness or emptiness, not taking care to ensure the mutual relationship requirements of both parties will be met. Too often we jump into relationships blindly, thinking romantic love or infatuation is *real* love. These types of love often are short lived because they often lack sustainability: one or both partners may be wanting that stage of love to last, and when the heat has left the relationship they become bored or feel unloved because the heightened chemical attraction has faded. Often people are seeking to return their lover to this former state and it is not possible, as people change over time back into their relaxed state and you get the *real* them. Conflict can start at this stage and if couples lack communication skills, the relationship dies. However, some partners don't give in to the relationship's death, blindly trying to return to their chemical high and infatuated state, leaving them open to staying in an unhealthy relationship.

An unhealthy relationship may have some, many or all these characteristics:

Closed or ineffective communication

- Unwillingness to talk over things that bug either you or them
- Ignoring your requests to talk
- Walking away when you bring up problems
- Using silence as a punishment
- One partner doesn't listen, or one does all the talking

...cont'd

GET OUT GET FREE

Closed or ineffective communication cont'd

- Dismissing each other's wants, needs or feelings
- One partner constantly blames everyone else, not taking responsibility or being accountable
- One partner attacks the other's behaviour or personality
- Twisting stories around
- Using your wounded feelings against you
- One or both partners avoid dealing with conflicts at all costs
- Lose-win on conflicts or problems
- Being judgemental
- Being closed to ideas
- Inconsistency and changing of goals without consultation
- Sneaky ways and manipulation
- Getting angry and worked up over little insignificant things
- Holding your errors and faults against you and bringing them up over and over again
- Badgering
- Nagging

Feeling unsafe

- Possessiveness
- Being coercive or forceful
- Insecurity
- Misery
- Addiction issues such as alcohol, drugs, work, sex and gambling

WHAT IS AN UNHEALTHY RELATIONSHIP

Dominating/lacks sharing

- Does not compromise
- Making plans without consulting you
- Pries into where you go, with whom, how long, etc.
- Expects you to give up your friends, family, co-workers to be with them
- Tells you what to do
- Is always in control
- When you feel good, they put you down
- Lies about their position or job
- Two-faced, hypocritical, backstabbing

Lacks commitment

- Sporadically available
- Lacks trust
- Tries to rush the relationship
- Blocks communication to work on any issue
- Committed to another person
- Not available to spend time together due to other commitments
- Emotionally unstable
- Insists on their freedom to come and go as they want, does not want to settle down or wants the freedom of many lovers
- Blames you for their unhappiness
- Unequal levels of commitment

GET OUT GET FREE

Inequality

- Giving more than you are receiving
- One partner doesn't think they are good enough or isn't comfortable with themselves
- They think they are too good
- Putting you on a pedestal
- Belittles you, your talents, and things that are important to you, either in private or in public
- Always wants to do it either only their way or only your way
- Does not think of you
- Too much flash
- Jealousy
- Lacks any friends (may have many acquaintances)
- Treats service persons (e.g. waiters, clerks) with disrespect
- Unequal power / abuse of power
- Lacks respect for the values of partner

Indifferences

- Not free to be yourself
- Attempting to fix/change/rescue/help them reach their full potential, as they aren't good enough
- Excluding friends that are different to your partner
- Lacking tolerance for the differences in each other

WHAT IS AN UNHEALTHY RELATIONSHIP

Lacks intimacy

- Cool and aloof
- Not comfortable touching or kissing
- Someone that wants "to sit in each other's lap" too frequently or for too long
- Withholds sex as a punishment
- Makes you do things sexually which you do not want to do
- Criticises your intimate parts or intimacy methods
- Constantly places work, gadgets, children or chores first
- Does not express feelings of love either sexually, affectionately or with words
- Does not display physical intimacy, with or without sex, including spontaneity, romance and affection in front of others

Partners lack individuality

- Melding of lives into one, no time apart
- Low self-esteem and confidence
- Lacks respect for your rights, differences and goals as an individual
- Lacking respect for each other's space

Lacks growth

- Takes too much care of you, to hold back your growth
- Over-concern for you (the rescuer)
- Does not want you to grow and leave them behind

GET OUT GET FREE

An unhealthy relationship needs attention as soon as is practical. When you attempt to bring up the issues that you are concerned about and you are stonewalled, dismissed or not taken seriously, this means your partner is not wanting resolution to the problem right then. Possibly time and thought processing is required by both parties after the initial discussion. If no resolution or agreement to move forward is made, the relationship may turn abusive or end.

In the next chapter we cover toxic and abusive behaviours, warning signs and signals.

Is my relationship toxic or abusive?

A toxic or abusive behaviour is where the needs of one or both partners of the relationship is neglected. Toxic behaviour can be overbearing, destructive and controlling, and may make the recipient fearful.

Stress reigns and it often feels like you are trying to resolve more than one problem at a time, like putting one fire out after another, yet never getting them all extinguished. An unhealthy relationship can quickly turn abusive without you even realising it, as your stress levels increase and your mood decreases from the ongoing strains in the relationship.

Being heard when expressing your concerns can be a daunting and relentless task, but because you are committed to the person you love you keep trying to get the relationship back into the previous loving state. Being blind to the changes occurring, and desperately needing the relationship to not end, you can try to maintain the status of the relationship by keeping your experiences to yourself.

- Most people don't realise that emotional, financial, sexual, social and spiritual abuse within relationships constitutes domestic violence. They may have the belief that only physical abuse is domestic violence. FDV (Family Domestic Violence) is when violence within a family unit is directed towards a partner (married or defacto), ex-partner, boyfriend or girlfriend, child/teenager, parent, carer, guardian, elder or extended family member.

- FDV occurs in families regardless of class, education, financial position, and cultural or religious background, and is against the law in Australia and many other countries. The perpetrators, who are usually, but not in all cases, influenced by behavioural problems stemming from childhood, mental illness, drugs or alcohol, control their victims through fear and coercion. FDV is a cultural and socio-economic problem clouded in stigma. This stigma of FDV means it is difficult for a victim to overcome and regain their sense of self, power and life. They often are worried that it is "all their fault" and outsiders wonder, "why they don't leave?" or, "why do they return?"

- One of the ways an abuser tries to gain control over you is to make you feel that your strengths are your weakness. The victim is never to blame. Even though alcohol and drugs can make the violence worse, they are not to blame. A perpetrator chooses to use violence against the victim. A classic example of these choices is where a husband can behave appropriately at work, taking orders from management and performing his work duties as required, yet abuses his partner when he returns home. This is clearly a choice that the husband makes about who he can abuse and who he cannot. Regardless of stresses, a perpetrator chooses how and towards whom to exercise their power and control.

Often FDV starts with emotional abuse and may lead into other forms of abuse. Emotional abuse is when your partner torments your mind and emotions. This can lead to you feeling like they have destroyed the core of who you are. These types of partners can also have a very charming side to their personality and many other people do not see their destructive or abusive side. Their behaviour can change drastically from one instant to another, and is a form of manipulation to gain control over you. Their inconsistent behaviour can make you feel like you are 'going mad', as your emotions are often used against you. You may find it difficult to ascertain what is causing the problems, because you are very busy trying to resolve one issue after another, as your partner shows loving behaviours towards you, then unloving ones. Emotional abuse is as real as physical abuse and can sometimes be more destructive than physical abuse over a period, becoming a form of brain washing that erodes at your self-worth and self-confidence.

- FDV tends to get worse over time and rarely decreases without proper support and intervention within the family unit. It has a negative impact on all the family members and it is proven that children who witness domestic violence towards a parent/caregiver/protector are affected in the same way as children who are the direct victims of violence.

- Hurt people, hurt people. Often perpetrators are hurt themselves and have developed behavioural patterns that involve gaining power and control over others in order to give themselves a sense of emotional security.

Stress is a natural response

Stress is a natural response to any threat or challenge. Some studies suggest that we inherit the tendency to be more susceptible to stress, whereas other studies say that we learn to feel stressed from a lifetime of stress responses.

Stress can be positive, good for you and can give you energy to get things done. An overload of stress can affect the way you think and feel, and will show in your behaviours, even without your conscious awareness. One person may cope relatively easily with a stressful situation, while another person may struggle. Long-standing stress can become problematic because it affects the way we think and feel. Ignoring it will not make it go away.

Often in an abusive or toxic relationship, we are very busy dealing with one problem after another, rarely having time in between to evaluate our general wellbeing, feelings or what we are thinking. We are never able to assess how many problems there have been and how long we've been trying to deal with them, therefore we don't see the impact the stress is having on us.

How do I feel today?

Ascertaining how we are feeling when under stress can be difficult because so much must be managed. We can bury feelings in order to cope. Putting our feelings aside to deal with the external drama is very common, and we can disassociate from our feelings. Here's some faces you can assess how you and others feel!

IS MY RELATIONSHIP TOXIC OR ABUSIVE

GET OUT GET FREE

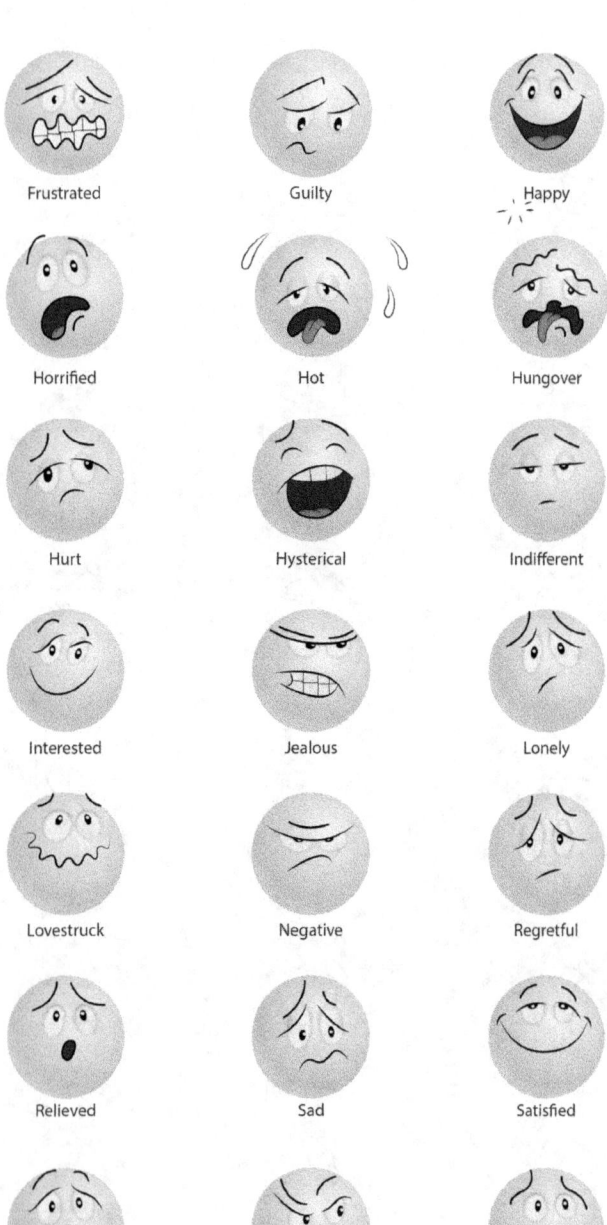

Stress symptoms

Here's a list of symptoms you may be experiencing when subjected to long-standing stress. Be totally honest with yourself if you are experiencing any of the following thoughts, feelings, behavioural or physical symptoms:

Thoughts
- I'm not happy
- I can't cope
- I can't think clearly
- What is there for the kids?
- I need a drink
- What can I do?
- I'm stuck
- How can I kill my partner?
- Why didn't I do something?
- Pessimistic thoughts
- When is this going to end?
- How much more of this can I take?
- I'm exhausted mentally
- I have no fun anymore
- I've lost my friends
- I've lost my family
- Suicidal thoughts
- No time for me
- Nightmares
- Disorientation
- Decision making difficulties
cont'd...

GET OUT GET FREE

Thoughts cont'd

- Slowed thinking
- Intrusive thoughts and images of the abusive incidents
- Can't tell anyone
- Forgetful/poor memory
- Indecisiveness
- Bad dreams or nightmares

Feelings

- Fear
- Anxiety
- Sadness
- Depression
- Numbness
- Feeling stupid
- Feeling vulnerable
- Hopelessness/Helplessness
- Irritability
- Frustration
- Anger directed at self or others
- Loneliness
- Feeling like running away
- Concentration difficulties
- Over-sensitivity
- Avoiding others
- Panic attacks
- Self-blame
- Feeling harassed

cont'd...

IS MY RELATIONSHIP TOXIC OR ABUSIVE

Feelings cont'd

- Afraid to tell anyone
- Scared of being alone
- Worried you caused it
- Scared of it increasing if you leave
- Worried what others will think
- No-one will believe you
- Can't focus on goals
- Difficulty seeing your future
- Abandoned by God/can't pray
- Feeling unprotected

Physical or behavioural

- Trying not to think
- Going for a walk
- Crying
- Working - over or under
- Withdrawing from activities
- Not making the effort to dress up
- Over/under eating
- Church/family/spiritual
- Alcohol/drugs/cigarettes
- Sharing with others
- Insomnia/sleep disturbance
- Difficulty relaxing
- Leaving/Returning
- Escape - going out/reading excessively
- Fatigue

cont'd...

Physical or behavioural cont'd
- Easily startled
- Shakiness
- Tiredness
- Tense or sore muscles
- Headaches
- Stomach upsets/nausea
- Skin reactions
- Repeated infections
- Shallow breathing
- Loss of libido or low libido
- Weight loss/gain
- Hair loss
- Hyper-alertness
- Fight, flight or submission

Anger as a signal

Anger is a powerful emotion and a great indicator that all is not well in your world. Anger is a natural response to being hurt; to our rights being violated; to our needs not being met; to emotional issues not being addressed; to our values, beliefs, ambitions being compromised, or being made to feel powerless. As explained in my book *Mind Chatter That Matters*, anger is a natural emotion and when used constructively it can bring about change in your life. When anger is distorted it is expressed through over-powerfulness, rage, hatred, frustration, bitterness, self-hatred, resentment, aggressiveness, powerlessness or hurt. You may lose your sense of inner authority and feel defeated, cheated and intimidated. When we start to express anger with these distorted behaviours, we are perceiving we have no authority to make changes to our lives.

Constructive ways to deal with anger and make changes:

- Finding some personal space
- Find ways you can release the anger to better understand why you're feeling it. E.g., exercise or physical activity, massage, cup of tea, bite or punch a pillow, writing or journaling, meditation, hobbies such as painting or drawing, crying it out to let it go, scream. All these methods help release the tension of anger.
- Seeking outside help with counselling, friends and family
- Taking responsibility for your own response to the situation
- Setting boundaries for what is making you angry
- Find something positive in your situation
- Positive self-talk
- How can you use this anger for change? Thinking outside the square?

When anger festers, it can turn out of control and is referred to as 'rage.' Some of the destructive ways of dealing with anger are:

- Behaviour that is inconsistent with your values
- Physical violence such as slamming doors, punching walls, furniture or people
- Careless driving
- Excessive use of food, alcohol, drugs, gambling or cigarettes

- Destroying property or memories
- Negative self-talk and put downs
- Bottling up feelings until they explode
- Thoughts of killing self or others

Attitudes and behaviours of people who use violence

Abuse is a psychological and physical game of power and control. It is not love. Abusers often share similar characteristics. They use controlling behaviours. These are some of the behaviours that constitute family and domestic violence and indicate that your partner may be abusing you:

Emotional abuse
- Says things to be hurtful and cruel
- Reducing your confidence with put downs
- Threats:
    - To kill, hurt or injure your pets, children or others
    - To destroy your property, finances and relationships with others
    - Suicide - taking their own life/yours/children
    - Not to expose the abuse
    - To your security - you will lose the children/house/money/family
    - Emotional blackmail
    - Indifference

cont'd...

IS MY RELATIONSHIP TOXIC OR ABUSIVE

Emotional abuse cont'd

- Giving orders
- Making a victim of themselves/negative self-talk
- Now or else directive
- Never give enough
- Humiliation
- Claiming you have mental problems
- Ridicule
- Put downs to make you feel stupid, mad or worthless
- Obsessive, possessive and jealous that you provoke his feelings
- Deliberately causing upsetting incidents that push you to the limit
- Criticising you as a parent or for being a working parent
- Being told you are not good enough
- Not allowing you to speak/respond
- Lying about what is happening
- Making you feel it is all your fault
- Uses promises to change and charm, gifts or affection if you want to leave
- Makes all the important decisions or undermines yours
- Minimalises your accomplishments or achievements
- Has sudden and extreme mood changes or is loving then abusive
- Projects their faults or blame onto you
- Wakes you to have an argument with you or to prevent you from sleeping
- Ridicules racial status

cont'd...

Emotional abuse cont'd

- Not free to be yourself
- Not allowing you to speak for yourself

Financial abuse

- Not free to spend for yourself
- Pushed to work for income
- Control of money
- Having to ask or be given an allowance
- Not knowing the full details of the income or financial status of the relationship
- Not following budget exactly
- Taking money without asking
- Taking back money
- Accounting for every cent you spend
- Not giving you enough money
- Forcing you to give up your money
- Keeping you short of money and basic needs
- Removing possessions from you
- Keeping the change when shopping for you
- Threatens immigration status

Social abuse

- Not being free to choose your own friends/family
- Isolates you from friends/family by not liking them
- Jealous over the time you spend with others
- Makes you account for every minute you spend away

IS MY RELATIONSHIP TOXIC OR ABUSIVE

Sexual abuse

- Being woken up for sex, forced to have sex, even when ill or soon after childbirth
- Being called frigid
- Rape, forcing sexual acts
- Telling you how to dress
- Complaints of never getting enough sex
- Sulking, anger or harassment to coerce you into having sex
- Unwanted sex but you comply to prevent outrage
- Accuses you of being unfaithful or blames you for their unfaithfulness

Spiritual abuse

- Forcing you to choose a religion or disallowing you from having one
- Sabotaging your beliefs by putting them down
- Using your beliefs to justify their behaviour
- Ridiculing your beliefs
- Uses your beliefs for forgiveness but not their repentance

Technology facilitated abuse

- Tracking your mobile phone
- Monitoring you through applications and banking accounts
- Threats and humiliation using social media
- Placing tracking devices in your vehicles
- Stalking, when used to monitor your whereabouts and company you keep

Physical abuse

- Intimidation
- Giving orders
- Stalking, including driving past, watching from a distance and unwanted gifts
- Stand-over tactics
- Choking, punching, hitting, slapping, kicking, pinching, holding back and pushing
- Slamming doors or punching walls/furniture
- Hiding keys to prevent you from leaving
- Alcohol or drug affected, or forces you to have drugs or alcohol
- Expects children to do things beyond their ability
- Cruelty to animals, children or others
- Withholds medical attention or intervention

Hisk risk triggers

Life events can cause stress and how they are managed in relationships can trigger FDV. These factors may put you at risk of on FDV:

1. Pregnancy or new birth of a child.
2. Misuse of drugs or excessive alcohol.
3. Isolation.
4. Financial issues.
5. Court orders or proceedings.
6. Abuse of pets and other animals.

7. Prior history of FDV in childhood or adulthood.
8. Isolation or barriers to seeking help.
9. Cultural rules for your specific gender.
10. Abusers access to or use of weapons.

Am I in an abusive relationship?

In this section, ask yourself these questions and answer them truthfully. Having a "yes" to any of these questions will give you an idea of what you may be facing in your relationship:

1. Do you feel nervous around your partner?
2. Do you feel scared to disagree with your partner?
3. Are you doing things to prevent your partner's negative behaviour?
4. Does your partner's jealousy prevent you from seeing people you love or enjoy being with, or does your partner accuse you of being with other possible partners or prevent you from doing things you want to do?
5. Do you do things to keep your partner happy at your own expense?
6. Are you criticised or humiliated, made to feel wrong, stupid, crazy or inadequate by your partner?
7. Do you feel that nothing you do is ever good enough in their eyes?
8. Do you feel pressured when it comes to sex?
9. Do you have to be careful of your behaviour around your

partner to avoid their anger?

10. Does your partner threaten to kill you, themselves or other people you care about?

11. Has your partner threatened you with violence or been violent in you and your children's presence?

12. Is your health, including mental health, suffering because of the daily stresses?

13. Is there an imbalance between work and life?

14. Is life feeling like constant work with no fun?

15. Is too much of your energy going into keeping your life in order?

16. Are your relationships with other people suffering, especially those with your children?

17. Do you rarely have time to breathe between dramas or are they increasing over time, escalating with severity?

18. Are you feeling overwhelmed and not able to achieve everything you need to?

19. Are you feeling irritated or frustrated a lot of the time?

20. Are you relying on other stimulants (alcohol, drugs, gambling) to numb the stresses in your life?

21. Do you ever feel so stuck you can't see your way out of your situation?

22. Are you slowly nose diving into depression or anxiety due to relationship stresses?

23. Are you having suicidal thoughts?

24. Are you feeling trapped?

Admitting that you are human and have every right to feel how and what you are feeling is the first step in acknowledging stress. You are normal and having a normal reaction to a stressful or abnormal situation. Your reaction may seem unreasonable but don't label yourself as 'crazy'.

Often perpetrators make excuses for their behaviours or blame you for making them react or for the bad things they do. You need to trust your instincts and understand that you cannot 'work it out' alone. You cannot save your partner at the expense of your own life, nor should you feel sorry for your partner. Believe in yourself and gather support for yourself from people you trust about what is happening to you and your children. You need to focus on getting help for you, not your partner at this stage. You need to establish safe ways to move forward, as explained in *Chapter 6 Stopping the Cycle of Violence*.

Here are some methods that might help reduce your stress levels:

- **Physical activity**, combined with alternate periods of relaxation, can help alleviate the stressful affects on your mind and body. Try to get out of your surroundings and exercise, go for a walk, go to the gym, swimming or even try relaxation – breathing slower as you picture your mind slowing down. Meditation can often help with stress – even if your mind chatter is trying to continue, persist.

- **Stimulants** can increase stress and your heartbeat. Try to cut out or cut down any stimulants you consume, such as coffee, tea, cola and energy drinks, alcohol, cigarettes and sugar. Overuse of drugs & alcohol can impair your ability to cope with long-standing and day-to-day stress.

- **Keep busy** to keep your mind off things.

- **Talk to people** – a problem shared can help you get a different perspective on your stresses. Ensure your confidant is supportive and gives you the space to share without judgement or instructions.

- **Make daily decisions**, even if they are minor, you will then feel some sense of control over your life. Under stress it is a good idea to avoid making major life decisions as your judgment may be impaired with the stress.

- **Time out** is needed to allow yourself some time to rest, sleep and think.

- **Feed yourself well** with good well-balanced meals and take supplements to add extra nutrition to your diet, as stress increases your nutritional requirements.

- **Journal daily** or as often as you can. This helps the observing part of your mind watch what is going on, as well as helps provide insight into what you are experiencing. Journaling is great to refer to as it shows you how you have grown out of problems and that not every day is the same. Time changes everything.

- **Ask for assistance** if you are having trouble understanding or coping with the stress. Asking for help or just a listening ear can make your stress load lighter. Sometimes articulating the stress and trying to find a solution can be difficult under extreme stress. Talking to a supportive and understanding person, especially if they are professionally trained, will give you a different perspective on your stress and its cause.

- **Regular check ins** to stop and see how you are feeling physically and emotionally as well as what you are thinking. This again gives you an insight that you can observe and allows you to strategically take actions or steps forward.
- **Results** come over time, not overnight. Take time to review your stress and realise that it probably didn't occur overnight, nor shall the reduction of stress. Take one day at a time.

Mental health issues

Learning more about mental health is something to consider if you are feeling unbalanced or suffering. Even if your abuser is the one suffering from a mental illness, learning about it will help you establish some of the reasons of why you are experiencing abuse. A significant number of Australians experience mental health problems and many sufferers are undiagnosed and/or unsupported.

Mental illness is very common. One in five Australians aged 16-85 (20%) experience a mental illness in any year. The most common mental illnesses are depression, anxiety and substance use disorder. These three types of mental illnesses often occur in combination. For example, a person with an anxiety disorder could also develop depression, or a person with depression might misuse alcohol or other drugs, in an effort to self-medicate. Of the 20% of Australians with a mental illness in any one year, 11.5% have one disorder and 8.5% have two or more disorders. Almost half of all Australians (45%) will experience a mental illness in their lifetime.[4]

The onset of mental illness is typically around mid-to-late adolescence, and the prevalence of mental illness is highest in the 18-24 age group. Data from the 2014 Mission Australia's Youth Survey showed that around one in five (21.2%) of young people (15-19 years old) met the criteria for a probable serious mental illness.[5] Common mental illnesses in Australians are: anxiety disorders (14%), depressive disorders (6%) and substance use disorders (5%).[6]

54% of people with mental illness do not access any treatment.[7] This is worsened by delayed treatment due to serious problems in detection and accurate diagnosis. The proportion of people with mental illness accessing treatment is half that of people with physical disorders.[8]

The table below is from the *Diagnostic and Statistical Manual (DSM) V* from the *American Psychiatric Association*, which clinicians and psychiatrists worldwide use to diagnose psychiatric illnesses. If you see some of these traits in someone, including yourself, seek professional help. Being able to overcome mental health issues is a rewarding challenge.

The table below shows the definition of each criteria from the DSM:

Antisocial/ Psychopathic	Inflated grandiosity and a pervasive patter of taking advantage of other people.
Avoidant	Inhibited from forming or maintaining relationships out of fears of humiliation and rejection.

Borderline	Show intense emotionality, impulsivity, internal feelings of emptiness and fears of rejection.
Obsessive-Compulsive	Hyper focused on details and are excessively stubborn, rigid and moralistic.
Schizotypal	Characterised by odd thinking and appearances or confused states.

You can find out more about mental illness at https://www.psychology.org.au

Your core beliefs

Learning about who you are and what you need to be happy is a fundamental process. It is essential to establish the 'you' that you may have lost in the process of abuse. Regular words can program our belief system when repeated often enough. Have you lost your sense of self because of your relationship? Have you been told that you are worthless, weak, stupid and unworthy? Over time you will start to believe what you are told, unless you resist listening to the words. Eventually your abuser will brainwash you to believe the repetitious abuse about your worth. What are you now thinking about who you are?

GET OUT GET FREE

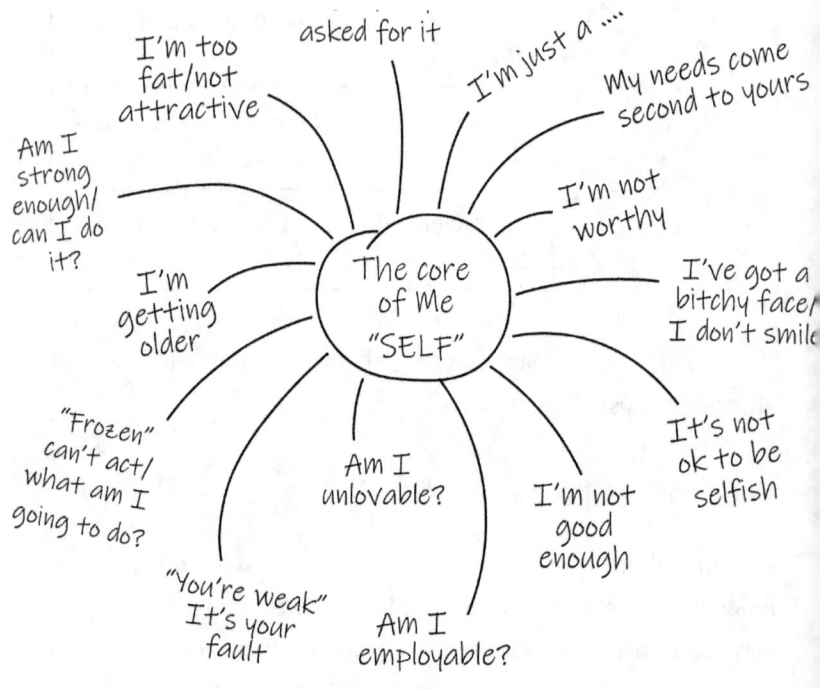

FDV & its impact

FDV is an epidemic problem within our Australian culture and all around the world. 'Domestic Violence' used to be synonymous with men's violence against their female partners in heterosexual relationships. However, it is now recognised that it also occurs where women use violence against their male partners; in gay, lesbian and trans-gender relationships; and may be directed at members of the family other than a partner. The term 'Family Domestic Violence' covers all these types of violence, which can be quite flexible and varied across cultures.

The Australian Government funded *National Plan to Reduce Violence against Women and their Children 2010-2022*[9] was released in 2011. Its goal is to allow *Australian women and their children live free from violence in safe communities*[10] and it aims to achieve a significant and sustained reduction in violence against women and their children.[11] The plan focuses on two main types of violence, FDV and sexual violence, through stopping violence before it begins, supporting the women who have experienced violence, stopping men committing the violence and building the evidence base to find what works to reduce FDV.

Australia's National Research Organisation for Women's Safety (ANROWS)'s paper *Violence Against Women: Accurate use of key statistics*[12] gathers collective information from the *Australian Bureau of Statistics (ABS)*, *Australian Institute of Health and Welfare*, *Australia's National Research Organisation for Women's Safety*. Authored by fourteen specialists in the area, it tells a brutal truth about violence in Australia.

Intimate partner violence is the greatest health risk factor (greater than smoking, alcohol and obesity) for women in their reproductive years.

- Intimate partner violence contributes more to the burden of disease (the impact of illness, disability and premature death) of adult women in their reproductive age (18-44 years) than any other risk factor. It contributes an estimated 5.1% of the burden for women aged 18-44 years.

- In 2010-12, approximately 41% of hospitalised assaults on women were perpetrated by an intimate partner.

Source: 2011 Australian Institute of Health and Welfare Burden of Disease Study (Ayre et al. 2016; Webster, 2016)

FDV & ITS IMPACT

Violence against women and their children results in major personal, government, and business costs.

- The total annual cost of violence against women and their children in Australia was estimated to be $22 billion in 2015-16.

    Source: 2015-16 Specialist homelessness services collection (Australian Institute of Health and Welfare, 2017)

- In 2015-16, 38% of all people requesting assistance from specialist homelessness agencies were escaping domestic or family violence (106,000 clients). This included 31,000 children aged under 15 and 66,000 women.

    Source: 2015-16 Specialist homelessness services collection (Australian Institute of Health and Welfare, 2017

Aboriginal and Torres Strait Islander women experience high rates of violence with significant health impacts.

- In the 12 months prior to the ABS survey, one in seven Aboriginal and Torres Strait Islander women had experienced physical assault. Of these, approximately a quarter indicated their most recent incident was perpetrated by a partner they have lived with.

    Source: 2014-15 National Aboriginal and Torres Strait Islander Social Survey (ABS, 2016)

- Intimate partner violence contributes an estimated 10.9% to burden of disease in Indigenous women aged 18-44 years. This is more than any other risk factor.

    Source: 2011 Australian Institute of Health and Welfare Burden of Disease Study (Webster, 2016)

Children often see or hear violence between their parents.

Since the age of 15:

- 50% (60,300) of women who had children in their care when they experienced violence by a current co-habiting partner reported that the children had seen or heard the violence.

- 68% (418,200) of women who had children in their care when they experienced violence by a previous co-habiting partner reported that the children had seen or heard the violence.

- Therefore, 65% of women who had children in their care when they experienced violence by a current or former partner, reported that the children had seen or heard the violence.

Source: 2016 Personal Safety Survey (ABS, 2017)

- In the four years from July 2010 to June 2014, child protection services in New South Wales, Victoria, and Western Australia received more than 335,000 reports of child maltreatment concerns, 16% of which included a concern about domestic violence.

Source: PATRICIA project (Humphreys & Healey, 2017; Slinky, Katz et al. 2017)

FDV & ITS IMPACT

> **Many women do not seek help about their experience of violence.**
>
> Of women who have experienced violence by a current partner since the age of 15:
>
> - Just over half (54% or 149,700) had sought advice or support about the violence they experienced.
> - 82% (225,700) had never contacted the police.
>
> Of women who have experienced violence by a former partner since the age of 15:
>
> - 63% (864,100) had sought advice or support about the violence they experienced.
> - 65% (888,100) had never contacted the police.
>
> Nine out of ten women who experienced sexual assault by a male (87% or 553,900) did not contact the police about the most recent incident.
>
> Of the 85,700 women who did contact the police, one quarter (27% or 23,500) reported that the perpetrator was charged.
>
> Source: 2016 Personal Safety Survey (ABS, 2017)

This data has fundamentally shaped Australia's understanding of FDV and the *National Plan to Reduce Violence against Women and their Children 2010-2022*[9] shall help shape how the Australian Government will manage the epidemic of violence. Without reporting violence, the government will misunderstand how prevalent violence is in our communities and the risk management strategies it requires to protect our people.

The *Family Protection Act* may vary slightly from state to state, but generally these acts all use the same definition for FDV. The *Victoria State Government Family Violence Protection Act 2008*[13] has clearly defined FDV as:

(a) behaviour by a person towards a family member of that person if that behaviour:

(i) is physically or sexually abusive; or

(ii) is emotionally or psychologically abusive; or

(iii) is economically abusive; or

(iv) is threatening; or

(v) is coercive; or

(vi) in any other way controls or dominates the family member and causes that family member to feel fear for the safety or wellbeing of that family member or another person; or

b) behaviour by a person that causes a child to hear or witness, or otherwise be exposed to the effects of, behaviour referred to in paragraph (a).

The barriers of escaping FDV in a relationship

FDV can have far reaching effects on victims, in particular if they flee the home with children, having minimal financial resources. This increases financial risk, poverty and financial insecurity. These fleeing victims are vulnerable to homelessness, severe social and personal disruption, including disruption to schooling, friendships and community support. Many victims choose safety over financial security when the violence is extreme and will survive on financial entitlements from various Government Departments. These victims often lack knowledge of what is available, and how the system could provide for them and protect them from a lifetime of financial hardship. Many still have to care for children and need to work full time to provide as a single parent family; which in turn impacts on their parenting capacity and increases stress and mental illness when dealing with an abuser's ongoing control and power.

FDV is often associated with increased rates of miscarriages and other pregnancy related injuries, including foetal death. It is common to first experience FDV during pregnancy.

Unfortunately, the ultimate fear for victims is death or being murdered due to FDV. Statistics show that over a 12-month period, on average, one woman is killed every week by a current or former partner. The *Australian Institute of Criminology* reports "Of the 185 domestic homicides throughout the 2008–10 period, 122 (66%) were sub-classified as intimate partner homicides, 22 (12%) as filicides (7 of which involved an infanticide; that is, the death of a child under 1 year of age), 20 (11%) as parricides and four (2%) as siblicide. The remaining 17 (9%) were classified as 'other' family homicides."[14]

Cultural and diverse groups should be embraced not by integrating them but intersecting with them. We should not blame or stigmatise specific cultures as it makes it more difficult for victims to speak up and seek the help they need. Victims within culturally diverse groups are impacted by male privilege, isolation, and many other barriers, such as challenges with language, information, financial support, legal systems (including police and court systems), and access to housing. When a victim is not an Australian Resident, they may perceive there to be limited options for financial support. These victims can feel they have nowhere to turn, as there may be little support within their culture to disclose the FDV or leave the relationship.

Victims with disabilities are twice as likely to experience FDV because abusers target victims who are less powerful and may not be able to communicate what is happening to them.

Chapter 6 Stopping the Cycle of Violence will explain how you can plan your escape, regardless of your culture or disability, and reach out for the protection and support you need so that you or your children do not become a statistic of FDV. *Chapter 7 Your Legal Rights* will assist you in asserting boundaries with your abuser and *Chapter 8 Moving Forward* will detail what resources are available to you if you are suffering FDV and where to seek the help you need.

- Keeping a diary of events and feelings is very helpful. It's a record of what you are encountering and reminds you that emotions come and go. Nothing stays the same every day and you have resources within and externally that can help you escape the situation.

Revise your relationship. What are some of the good things about your relationship? What are some of the not so good things? What are some of the ways your partner has been abusive to you? How has it made you feel? What has your partner gained through their behaviour towards you?

- Once you realise that your relationship is in serious trouble

FDV & ITS IMPACT

and you are at further risk of abuse, you may feel angry, hurt, trapped and disappointed, and it is natural to grieve for your relationship and life you've imagined with your partner. You may also grieve for the former self you feel you have lost.

The journey through grief begins with *shock*, where you can't believe what has happened to you and you may feel numb. Next comes *denial*, as you don't believe it could have happened to you or your family. Then you get really *upset*, feel heartbroken and may cry a lot or for a long time. After that you feel *sad* and unhappy, heavy hearted, choked up inside, down in the dumps but with reduced crying. Feeling *alone* comes next: you'll feel like no one else has been through the same experience, or feels the same, or knows how you feel. *Guilt* follows, because you feel lousy, thinking that maybe you somehow caused it, or that you may have been able to prevent everything from happening. *Anger* arrives when you hate what has happened, hate your partner, maybe even yourself. The *wishing* stage is when you begin to remember only the good times you once had and you wish they would come back. Getting *back to normal* is when you start to feel less upset about things and sometimes you begin to feel ok, and feel maybe life can go on again. *Acceptance* has occurred when you acknowledge you don't feel happy about the FDV but realise that is has happened and you no longer pretend it hasn't happened. *Moving on* is the point where you've accepted the situation and realised that life does go on for you and that you can possibly feel happy again.

The impact of FDV has far reaching consequences and there are many factors to weigh up before establishing if you should stay or leave, and when to plan the safe exit. See *Chapter 6 Stopping the Cycle of Violence* for more information on the resources you may need to review before making the decision to exit your FDV relationship.

Defining trauma

My dictionary defines trauma as a deeply distressing or disturbing experience. Trauma can be the stuff of everyday life, such as divorce, accidents, health problems and losing a loved one through bereavement; yet the definition is wide enough to include the extreme trauma of war, torture, rape and genocide. People react differently to trauma. The American Psychiatric Association defines *Acute Stress Disorder* and *Post Traumatic Stress Disorder (PTSD)* as conditions that can occur in people who have experienced or witnessed a traumatic event. About half of people with *Acute Stress Disorder* go on to have *Post Traumatic Stress Disorder.* These disorders can be triggered by car or serious accidents, violent personal assault, repeated attacks, rape or mass shootings, natural disasters, war and terrorist attacks. Women are twice as likely as men to have *PTSD*. The sufferers relive the events regularly; have flashbacks or nightmares; feel sadness, fear or anger; and feel numb or detached from themselves or estranged from others. They may avoid situations or people that remind them of the trauma or may have strong negative reactions to something as ordinary as a loud noise or accidental touch. For example, *PTSD* could occur in an individual learning about the violent death of a close family member. It can also occur as a result of repeated exposure to horrible details of trauma, and police officers sometimes develop it after being exposed to details of child abuse cases.[15]

In order to protect yourself and your children, it is paramount you understand the effects of trauma and the impact of FDV.

Mental illness - signs and signals

It is important for each and every one of us to take care of our mental health. Living with a person with mental health issues can cause mental health issues in others, as issues can affect the entire family. Mental illness can't be seen in sufferers unless you diagnose patterns of behaviour, and the symptoms it produces may be put down to stressful life events and experiences.

Here's a list of 9 signs of mental illness.[16] These are not shown to help you diagnose a mental health problem, but to indicate that there might be a good reason to obtain more information from a trained doctor (GP), psychologist or healthcare professional:

1. Feeling anxious or worried
2. Feeling depressed or unhappy
3. Emotional outbursts
4. Sleep problems
5. Weight or appetite changes
6. Being quiet or withdrawn
7. Substance abuse
8. Feeling guilty or worthless
9. Changes in behaviour or feelings.

It is imperative that people seek help if they've been thinking negatively for a long period of time and their feelings are beyond feeling 'blue' every now and then. Counselling is extremely helpful to give you insight into why you are feeling the way you do.

In *Chapter 8 Moving Forward*, you will learn where to seek help and recover from the trauma that you may have experienced.

Children of FDV

Many people don't understand the effects of FDV on children and the deep emotional harm they encounter and can suffer because it is part of their lives. These children too can suffer from mental health issues that go undiagnosed their entire lives or they may develop personality disorders later in life. Children exposed to trauma are deeply affected; they may develop coping mechanisms, or may lack the confidence or communication skills needed to develop into healthy, happy, well-adjusted children, adolescents and adults.

Even when children do not experience the violence directly, they are usually aware of it, as they are alert to the obvious tension, distress and fear that their parents are experiencing. A home should be a 'safe' haven for all that live within its walls, and when the safety within those walls is marred by cruelty and fear, the children no longer feel safe.

One Victoria study of police statistics found a "disturbing feature of family violence is the presence of your children", with under five-year olds witnessing 65% of domestic disputes involving threat or use of a gun, 79% of disputes involving another weapon, usually a knife, and 67% of disputes where property was damaged (Wearing, 1992).

Children are affected and experience FDV in many ways. They

FDV & ITS IMPACT

may:

- Experience the violence directly or indirectly, as abusers often abuse their children too. This also includes sexual abuse to a child.

- Become indirect victims of physical injury whilst trying to protect a victim or a weapon being used on a victim. Infants can be injured when being held. Unborn infants can also be harmed.

- Be used as a hostage to control one of the parents.

- Have their relationship with the victim undermined by the abuser denigrating or expressing a negative opinion of them.

- Be forced to watch or participate in the violence.

- Be made to make a choice about whether to become the victim or identify with the aggressor and begin to act out the violent and aggressive behaviour towards others.

- Experience the fear of their parent being victimised.

- Robbed of their sense of personal safety, as their security and the familiarity of their belongings or pets is destroyed.

- Become victims of emotional and psychological trauma likened to PTSD, which can be far worse if unacknowledged.

- Become fearful and withdrawn, as they see the whole world as a hostile place and may become bullied by other children.

- See themselves as the blame for the abuser's anger and aggression.

- Feel helpless or ashamed if they don't intervene or prevent the abuse.

- Take on the responsibility of protecting the victim and step up as the parent.
- Have difficulty in concentrating at school as they have learnt how to 'switch off' to cope with the violence at home.
- Lack support from the victimised parent, who is also traumatised by the violence.
- Have physical symptoms such as bed wetting, stress related illness such as headaches and stomach pains, speech difficulties such as stuttering, and sleep difficulties such as nightmares, or even regression such as thumb sucking.
- Withdraw from people and events.
- Experience separation anxiety, be depressed or feel suicidal.
- Experience body image and eating problems.
- Be cruel to animals.
- Begin to use drugs or alcohol to cope with the stresses of the violence
- Learn poor conflict resolution skills, repress their feelings and have decreased empathy towards others.
- Run away from home or end up homeless.
- Have an inability to form stable intimate adult relationships later in life.

Children tend to normalise violence if it is experienced regularly. The repeated episodes of violence make violence seem acceptable, and children commonly feel responsible for the violence. They may blame their siblings or the other parent for the violence, not understanding the abuser is responsible. Through be-

FDV & ITS IMPACT

ing exposed to violence by their role models, children's beliefs about how relationships operate are influenced. They may begin to accept that it is ok to abuse your partner, including hitting them, and that violence is an effective way to solve problems or win an argument. They don't learn consequences, if any, for violence. If the violence is perpetrated by the father, they learn that women are weak, and men are strong or vice versa. Ironically, they believe that inequality in relationships is normal, that it is possible to love and inflict pain at the same time and it is an effective way to relieve stress. However, not all children who grow up with violence will grow up to abuse others.

Children feel pressured to maintain the family's secret of the violence. They may avoid bringing friends home or be unable to engage in social events due to their isolation. Death threats are a child's biggest concern, as they believe that the abuser shall carry them out should the violence be exposed or the victims leave the home.

Coping with FDV as an adult is difficult, but once you see your children suffering it makes you respond from your parental protective nature. Unfortunately, the majority of victims leave their abusers once they witness the detrimental effects the violence is having on their children and rarely beforehand.

Children need a strong and positive view of themselves and this is role modelled through their parents/guardians and peers. Children need a sense of meaning and direction in their lives and to feel powerful as they move into their adult lives of responsibility and independence. Giving your child the best opportunity to live a safe and happy life is a parent's first priority. Using this priority and becoming aware of the detrimental effects that FDV is having on your children will motivate you to gain the support you need to stop the violence.

Remember children need to learn respectful relationships that are non-violent. This is especially true during adolescence, often a stressful time when they may swing between wanting comfort from you and then seeking some independence. Discuss how violence is a destructive way to solve upsets and differences in a relationship, and make it clear that violence is a choice, not an option. Give your children a safe environment to express their feelings and encourage or show them ways to do so. Encourage your children to be successful and strong in healthy ways such as in education, sport, music, friendships and employment. Encourage them to follow their dreams and goals. Continue to work at keeping a close relationship with your children to maintain a close and supportive bond between you.

Understanding the cycle of violence helps you to see how you may be entrapped. Making decisions is the next step to keeping you and your children safe. In *Chapter 6 Stopping the Cycle of Violence* you will learn ways to exit the violent relationship and where to seek help. *Chapter 7 Your Legal Rights* will give you the guidance for staying safe and setting firm boundaries legally.

When to report children experiencing FDV

A child is a victim of FDV if they have witnessed or been directly or indirectly involved in violence. You should first visit your doctor and have the event documented and have your health professional ring and report the abuse to your State Government's Child Protection Department. You must insist that they make the report. Do not leave it as one incident, one report. Ensure you also report child abuse to the department as well as any other member of the public that may have witnessed the violence on at or in the presence of the child.

Reporting child abuse is crucial; regardless of the degree of the violence, once reported it is documented and forms a case within the department and mounts evidence against an abuser. When a report is made, the department acts on the case, depending on the level of abuse and the number of reports for the child. When FDV is reported via a police report, a restraining order of the Local Court (your State Government court) is placed and it becomes an automated reported case. The Family Court (Federal Government) has access to the department's reports. Please refer to *Chapter 7 Your Legal Rights* for an explanation of each court system.

Education departments within each state are obligated to report a child's physical and sexual abuse, as are health care professionals. Often an abuser will have several reports before the violence level increases. The department acts where another party, preferably another responsible family member or the other parent, is recommended to remove the child from the abuser and seek legal advice. Therefore, it is paramount to not defer the child abuse report, even if the child has only witnessed violence. Do not wait a day or two. You may think that the violence shall stop if you appease the abuser, but it is often the beginning of long-term abuse. Abuser's rarely change their behaviour of power and control without taking accountability and responsibility for their actions and obtaining professional help.

Do not dismiss the needs of your child when it comes to them being directly involved or witnessing violence. Parental neglect is also considered to be child abuse. Ensure you report every event, even if the other parent neglects your child's basic requirements such as dietary needs, medical needs or sleep.

Unfortunately, when child sexual abuse occurs the perpetrator is usually someone known and trusted by your child. It must also be included in this section. As horrific as it is, child sexual abuse includes an adult or older adolescent using the child for sexual stimulation, penetration, fondling, indecent exposure, grooming, exposure to inappropriate acts or material not appropriate for their age, such as pornography or sexual interactions. Children often exhibit overly sexualised behaviour when they have been sexually abused and this must be taken seriously. The research on the longer-term impact of child sexual abuse indicates that there may be a range of negative consequences for mental health and adjustment in childhood, adolescence and adulthood.[17]

There is also a considerable overlap between physical, emotional and sexual abuse, and children who are subject to one form of abuse are significantly more likely to suffer other forms of abuse. Mullen and colleagues (1996) found women with histories of child sexual abuse had over five times the rate of physical abuse and were three times as likely to also report emotional deprivation.[18]

When dealing with a first instance of abuse involving a child you may be too embarrassed to admit the violence, or too overwhelmed or scared to share, report or take preventative steps to stop further abuse. However, you should always report any form of child abuse, as it will provide you with substantial evidence that may later be reviewed by authorities, and having that evidence properly recorded will assist you immediately or in the future. Please do not disregard how imperative it is that you report the violence. As *Chapter 7 Your Legal Rights* explains, you need evidence to support your case should you require the use of the legal system to establish the abuse and set boundaries to protect you and your children. *Chapter 8 Moving Forward* shares where you can find assistance and support when you need to report or seek advice on what you and your children are going through.

Stockholm syndrome

You probably have heard of hostages becoming close to their captors as a survival strategy. Stockholm syndrome is the name given to this psychological alliance that results from a bond being formed between prisoner and captor during the intimate time spent together. The alliance seems irrational, as the hostages develop positive feelings towards their captors and even believe in the humility of their captors. It is believed to develop where the hostage's survival need is stronger than their need to hate their captor and is a defence mechanism of the ego mind under immense stress.

Essentially it is where the hostages' likelihood of survival increases when they are terrorised into 'helpless, powerless, and submissive' states. Actions and attitudes similar to those suffering from Stockholm syndrome have also been found in victims of sexual abuse, human trafficking, discrimination, terror, and political and religious oppression.[19]

This syndrome could develop for you or your children as result of a FDV relationship, and significant psychiatric or psychological counselling is required to recover. You should take this condition seriously and seek advice if any symptoms develop.

The cycle of violence

Being in a FDV relationship means you go through many highs and lows. As you attempt to forgive and forget, another cycle may erupt, leaving little time for rest and recuperation. Every time you give a little more to appease your abuser, you teach them how to treat you. Once you tolerate a certain behaviour, you have indicated that it's ok for them to repeat that behaviour. When you fight back, demand boundaries and respectful behaviours, the other person often turns the requests back on you, changes subjects to criticise something you've done that has upset them, or dismisses you altogether. Gas-lighting is a common tactic used by abusers: they tell blatant lies, deny they said something (even with proof), use things that are important to you against you (such as your children, or your worth at work or within a family), turn the heat up over time (telling lie upon lie to confuse you), are incongruent with their words and actions (what they say and do don't match) and then praise you to distract you from focusing on the manipulation.

THE CYCLE OF VIOLENCE

Arguments are common in relationships but learning to listen to another's point of view and accept the differences is a natural part of communication and acceptance. After the *Integration* stage of a relationship, FDV relationships tend to have arguments with win-lose results, as your differences start to become apparent, and when communicating your needs your words are twisted or you are misunderstood, unheard, or your needs are denied. Because the love has been so intense and undeniable, you may continuously attempt to return to the earlier stages of your relationship, whilst ignoring the warning signs of FDV. It is common for people to put the need of having the relationship above their emotional safety, and are often unaware of the subconscious decision to not self-protect. This can be triggered by several reasons, including previous abuse from childhood, sexual or emotional neglect, or learned patterns in relationships. Both partners must make conscious decisions to maintain, invest in and stay in a relationship, and be accountable and responsible for the health of the relationship. Healthy relationships with good communication skills, where partners listen, adapt, compromise and support the differences in each other, usually resolve arguments with a win-win result.

The *Cycle of Violence* model was developed by Lenore Walker in the US in 1979 and it can help you recognise FDV and also explain why you have stayed in your FDV relationship. It refers to a repeated cycle of dangerous acts of violence. The pattern, or cycle, repeats and can happen many times in a relationship. It can worsen by nature over time, and the behaviour of an abuser can vary dramatically, leaving you confused about the health of your relationship.

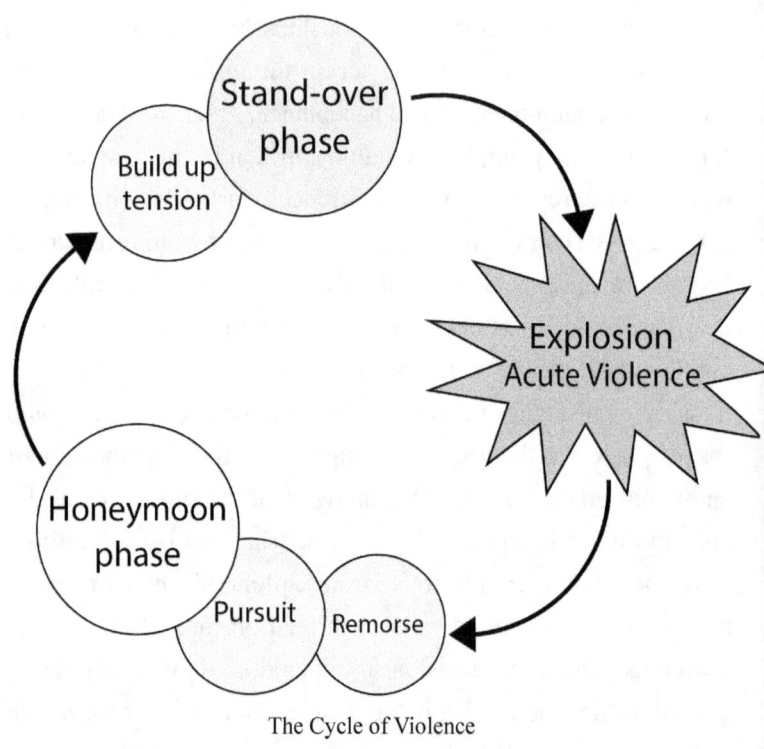

The Cycle of Violence

Phase 1 - Build up and stand over

Initially you may feel that you are just having arguments. However, this phase is where tension between partners increases, as does the use of verbal, emotional or financial abuse. This is where the abuser starts controlling your behaviours and response. The phase may last hours, days or weeks, and builds from stresses of daily life, such as conflict over money, children, marital issues, misunderstandings, illness, or employment. In this phase of the abuse you may feel ignored because you don't have the same view, or threatened because you won't comply or agree.

THE CYCLE OF VIOLENCE

The abuser may be angry, act as if wronged or be self-righteous. In this phase you may start to feel:

- Unloved and no longer cared about.
- Like you are dependent on your partner for your happiness.
- Bewildered at how angry they are getting over so little.
- You are never heard.
- Scared that they will target the children if you don't do what they want.
- You want to fix things to get the relationship back to normal.
- Pressured to appease the abuser.
- Fearful of loss of your relationship, home, money, life, security etc.
- You have limited options.
- Isolated, stressed, embarrassed and withdrawn.
- Angry, anxious, sad or depressed.
- Anxious to keep the peace and comply with their requests.
- That you need to nurture the abuser to reduce their anger.
- As if you do all the 'giving' and they do all the 'taking.'
- Concerned for your wellbeing and security.
- Concerned that they will follow through with their threats.
- Afraid that their anger will escalate, and you may be physically hurt, or your things may be damaged.
- As if you are constantly trying to fix the problems and nothing you do stops the abuse.

- Aware that triggers outside that are affecting your relationship but you can't change them.
- As if you need to make excuses for the abuser's behaviour.
- Blamed for all the problems and the abuser's crazy behaviour.
- Defensive.
- Eager to get the phase over and done with, knowing that the next phase is coming regardless.
- That no-one would believe you, because abusers hide their abuse behind closed doors to avoid being held accountable to others outside of the relationship.

Phase 2 - Acute violence or explosion

This undeniable explosive phase, with everything escalating, involves abusive outbursts of deliberate desire to intimidate, hurt or kill. There will be threatening or actual physical force, such as slapping, kicking, punching, choking, grabbing, rape, beating, restraint, spits, use of weapons, throwing objects, screaming, or slamming doors. The abuser will also be verbally and psychologically abusive, and there is nothing you can do to prevent this behaviour.

An abuser feels a reduction of tension once anger is released, and may express reasons for the explosive behaviour such as, "You deserved it", "Why would you make me do this to you?", "You pushed me too far", etc. This phase is used to dominate the you, and in this phase you may:

- Feel trapped, helpless or numb.

THE CYCLE OF VIOLENCE

- Submit helplessly.
- Protect yourself and your children any way you can.
- Try to calm your abuser down.
- Try to reason with your abuser.
- Try to call the police.
- Try to leave.
- Fight back with verbal or physical retaliation.

Phase 3 - Honeymoon

After the explosion of phase two the abuser may feel, or claim to feel, remorseful or guilty. They may not understand why you are still angry or concerned, and may forget about the degree of abuse you experienced. Apologies are accompanied by promises that it won't occur again. This phase is often characterised by affection, gifts or assurances that the abuser will do their best to change or give up drugs or alcohol or whatever the person claims has caused the abuse. They may be fearful that the victim may call the police or that the abuse will be exposed. Suicidal threats or concerns can increase in this phase, as the abuser may feel so remorseful and out of control because of the damage they have done, or fearful that they may lose their partners. They may ask forgiveness, declare their undying love for you, or shower you with attention. Some abusers walk away like nothing has happened, or ignore that there has been an incident. However, the honeymoon phase is characterised by a sense of calm and peace following the explosive phase. Eventually the honeymoon phase disappears and the cycle starts building up to start phase one again. In the honeymoon phase you may:

- Feel relieved their anger has subsided.
- Feel hopeful that it won't repeat.
- Feel happy that the abuser is loving again.
- Feel guilty that you may have contributed to their anger.
- Forgive them because of their childhood experiences.
- Forgive them because they have outside stresses.
- Make excuses for their behaviour.
- Try to talk about future incidents and ways to manage them.
- Set up counselling for the abuser or both of you together.
- Agree to stay in the relationship or take the abuser back.
- Drop legal proceedings you may have started.
- Be concerned about the abuser committing suicide.

Denial of the severity of the abuse prevails as intimacy increases and both partners feel happy. Both want to continue the relationship, ignoring the possibility of repeating the cycle again. However, the effect of broken promises and repeated cycles of abuse leave the victims feeling worn down and confused. Abusers are so convincing, while victims are eager to resolve the problems in the relationship and at the same time desperately need the relationship to return to its former happy state. The victims choose the needs of the abuser and relationship over their own need for safety and security. Until the victim becomes aware of the cycle, they are stuck and may be unable to seek help to escape the relationship.

THE CYCLE OF VIOLENCE

Awareness of the cycle

It is common for a victim to become powerless when they gain an awareness of the cycle of abuse they have endured. Victims can often feel terrified of finally taking a stand and making changes to their lives to ensure their own and their children's mental and personal safety. This powerlessness is often a result of the abuser's repetitive verbal put downs and criticisms – victims have come to believe this criticism is true. They often feel as they have no mental resources to combat the issues within the relationship anymore, nor the strength to escape. Being torn between your heart's emotions of needing the abuser to change and love you back, and the need to save your life and mind, is a difficult process for the victim to come to terms with.

Mental illness may have already affected them, and they may be suffering from anxiety or depression. They may have felt like they have had to keep the relationship together for so long, that they feel their sense of self has disappeared and there is nowhere to turn. They may be too embarrassed to tell anyone about the ongoing abuse and how long they have tolerated it for.

When the realisation hits that the relationship is one of abuse, they feel so unimportant, deceived and hurt. Victims realise that their partner may not love them at all, and that the relationship is more for their abuser's benefit than theirs. They are stuck somewhere between "I am not safe" and "I still love them".

You must acknowledge the love you once had and the amount of effort you have placed into the relationship to return it to its loving state. This is the key. You need to see how all the effort you placed into the relationship and that has gone unnoticed. You may feel stupid to have invested so much for so little return. You may feel guilty for not loving yourself first. You realise that you have put the abuser's needs above your own. You realise that the abuser can't love to the extent that you can and that they can't express and show love with the depth that you can. You realise that they are broken. And that you now feel broken.

Unconscious need for love

When conceived, we are born in a family with no awareness or choice of how that family unit is going to contribute to our life.

Regardless of the type of family unit – a loving family, adopted family, foster family, or a child welfare care home of any culture – we adapt to the basic needs of love, food, shelter and protection. We are unaware of how we learn to behave to ensure our survival within our family unit and it's cultural rules.

We are taught by the rules and guidance from our caretakers how we must act and behave to receive their love, nurturing and basic survival requirements – such as being fed, watered, clothed and housed from birth. This forms our perception of how the world works and what we believe that our world is and we continue to follow these rules that govern our behaviours in order to receive love, acceptance and our survival within the unit and the outer world.

In our childhood and teenage years we adapt to these influences from parents, grandparents, guardians, siblings, teachers and peers. Soon we learn that if we don't behave in ways expected of us, we feel the punishment of the withdrawal of their love, respect and support. This creates pain, and to avoid the pain, as well as survive, we learn to behave. It is from this experience that we perceive that our love, nurturing and basic survival is external to us and that these people have the power to remove it at any time. This unconscious process is why we may perceive an emptiness when love leaves us as we believe that love is outside of us and we continue to recorrect our behaviour to receive that love and nurturing.

By role modelling behaviours to us, our families and friends teach us many things; to love, express emotions, take care of each other; how to wash, cook, clean, budget, maintain a home, work etc. From this role modelling, we internalise these roles and learn to take care of ourselves throughout our childhood. adolescence and adulthood by adapting to the expectations of our role models. Some role models succeed in teaching us well, however, many fail. How we internalise role modelling, is how we learn to self-parent. Our own self-parenting voice that is internalised becomes our rules, beliefs, morals and integrity.

How many of these role models stop and tell you how competent you are to self-parent? Very little caregivers remind us of our capacity to see what we have absorbed from their teachings, but are quick to criticise, reject and disapprove to recorrect our behaviour where we haven't learnt. Most caregivers constantly point out the areas that we fail in, and don't reassure us that we can healthily self-parent most areas of our life. They don't recognise the attributes we have taken on and the areas where we do in fact, succeed, and often fail to acknowledge theses successes. Unfortunately, these repetitive negative messages train your belief systems and we also fail to acknowledge how we have learnt to self-parent and self-love. Rather than acknowledging our own successes, we blindly and constantly seek their and others approval due to feeling like we are failures in most avenues of our life.

It is a parent or caregiver's natural disposition to encourage you to be your best person. However sometimes they lack the ability to support us in ways we need. They may be off target because they are playing the role they believe a parent should play. That perception is heavily influenced by their own role models, experiences, culture, current mental health and life situation. They can fail us, we can internalise the failure and go on to lack self-parenting skills in many aspects. Unconscious patterns of the need for love, approval and acceptance can become ingrained. We will then embark on a lifelong task of trying to get others to love us, regardless of the efforts we make to seek the love, acceptance and reassurance we need.

When your role models demonstrate how to gain all your basic needs, you unconsciously internalise how to love, nurture others, give and take, support and provide for yourself first. Then you express and do those things for others. Not being aware of your own ability to self-support and self-love makes us reach out for love outside of ourselves, perceiving that love is external. However, love is internal as you cannot give what is not inside you, nor can you recognise what others are offering. You do not require love to be given to you, as you have already learned how to love from your role models.

You are <u>in fact</u> loving and love is a natural disposition of every human being. We are unconscious to, that love is within us as we are brainwashed that love is outside and we must constantly seek to gain it. This is the power of the ego mind, constantly striving to gain love, because it perceives it is nothing without love and control. Without everyone else filling up the empty void it perceives, it will strive relentlessly to gain love at any cost, sacrificing your mental health, wellbeing and safety, because it perceives that without the love, acceptance and approval from others, death will result. Therefore, the ego mind sabotages you into the belief that you must tolerate anything to gain that love. That is until you acknowledge your ability to self-love and self-parent.

It is from this unconscious need of love and acceptance that victims blindly and continuously ignore their own need for safety and security because they lack awareness of their own internalised self-love and self-acceptance. This is the double bind that victims find themselves in. The need for external love, versus the need to instinctually survive.

Once victims become aware that the relationship is unsafe because it threatens their physiological instinctual need for survival and avoidance of physical death, they are confronted by the unconscious need to obtain the external love they require to emotionally survive.

There is a perception of impending death arising from the unconscious ego mind and also a threat of death from physical and psychological torment. Two different areas of the brain are in conflict, both of them fighting for survival. This confusion causes immense stress. The possible loss of love, which means death to the ego or the possible loss of life, means death to our instinctual need of survival.

When you learn love is internalised and that you have the power to self-love, self-protect and self-parent, you can start to choose to escape the ongoing repetitive abusive cycles you have endured. Finally the unconscious mind wakes up. The ego mind will often attempt to return victims to the need for love, when the physiological threat of death has deminished or removed. This is why victims return to the empty promises of an abuser, believing that they can and will change.

Outsiders, not understanding this process, can often further victimise through a biased view of the torment that a victim is facing. Judgement is something victims are unable to cope with at this stage. They require support, understanding, guidance and love.

If you find yourself in this delimma, seek out someone who is non-judgemental, preferably a trained professional who can give you the guidance you need.

Cultural barriers

Depending on your culture and its rules, you may have inner conflict of your human rights versus your dire need to still fulfill your sense of belonging to your family culture's community and it's rules. Australia is a welfare culture that focus on the 'self' rather than 'culture rules' to provide freedom for each individual. Gaining your sense of *self* versus the requirement to be subservient to needs of another, be that an individual, family or culture is paramount is obtaining freedom from FDV.

Sadly over 70% of females in the world are victims of FDV and between 40-70% of these countries are murdered by their close partner.

Culturally and linguistically diverse (*"CaLD"*) people are more susceptible to FDV depending on the rules of subordination with the culture and their 'harmful cultural practices.' Immigrants and

THE CYCLE OF VIOLENCE

their family members living in Australia (regardless of birth in Australia or another country), are taught their own culture and it's rules of maintaining honour within the group. The pressure to follow and sustain the honour of the family/culture is immense and often unforgiving.

FDV victims within the CaLD community are often victimised barbarically threatening their mental and physical wellbeing by the culture with arranged or forced marriage (including children), female genital mutilation, honour killings or punishment to conform it's members. Sadly FDV tends to be extremely under reported in the CaLD community groups because of the need to conform or belong to their culture's collective sense of community rather than focus on their sense of self or self preservation. The rules are often based on men's punative right to control a woman as property by choosing their sexual and social choices. CaLD women are often treated as owned by the male members.

These victims face many fears such as:

- Immigration issues such as pending visa or residency status and fear of deportation, including ability to work or access to government financial support, education and benefits.
- Language barriers - may not understand that interpreters and translators are available and don't need their family to perform these roles.
- Community awareness, reaction and lack of family support and believe their partner may abduct their children to another country.
- Religious beliefs such as ability to divorce in Australia.
- Fears of our police system and justice system including

the family law.
- Lack of knowledge of general human rights.

In Australia, regardless of a victim's visa, residency or citizenship status, there is support to provide for a victim of FDV. Centrelink have payments that will support a victim even without a visa or residency status to prevent a victim being caught up in ongoing violence. There are also services that help a victim obtain a special visa to assist them if they are under a current visa application which is tied to their abuser from being trapped in ongoing FDV.

There are many reasons why FDV victims don't disclose the violence. They may not be aware they are being violated, won't be believed, may be judged or criticised, not supported to leave or confidentiality with their issues, think they are to blame, fear of being judged or criticised and may have even experienced negative consequenses from support services and the abuser

There are insurmountable dilemmas in leaving an abusive relationship. Outlined in the next chapter are the different risks that you may encounter and the possible solutions.

But before you start reading the next chapter, review the *Power and Control Wheel*[20] and the *Equality Wheel*[20] diagrams in the next pages to remind yourself of the differences in the types of behaviours of healthy and unhealthy relationships. You can find more wheels at https://www.theduluthmodel.org/wheels including *Using Children Post Separation*, *Abuse of Children* and *Nurturing Children*.

THE CYCLE OF VIOLENCE

Power & Control Wheel

The Duluth *Power & Control Wheel* stipulates the female gender, however it applies to all genders.

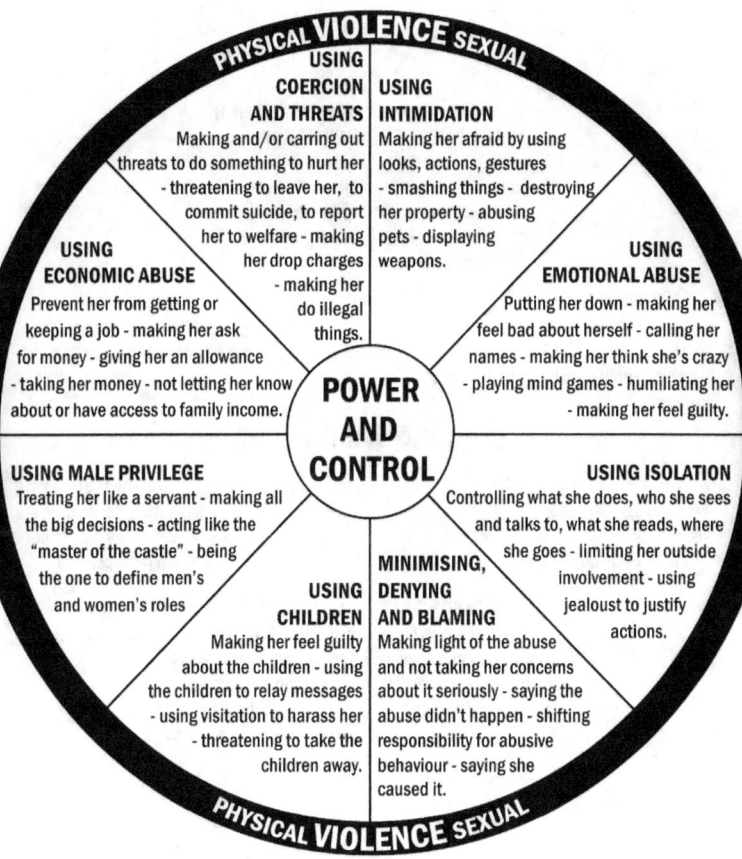

Figure from.theduluthmodel.org

GET OUT GET FREE

Equality Wheel

The Duluth *Equality Wheel* stipulates the female gender, however it applies to all genders.

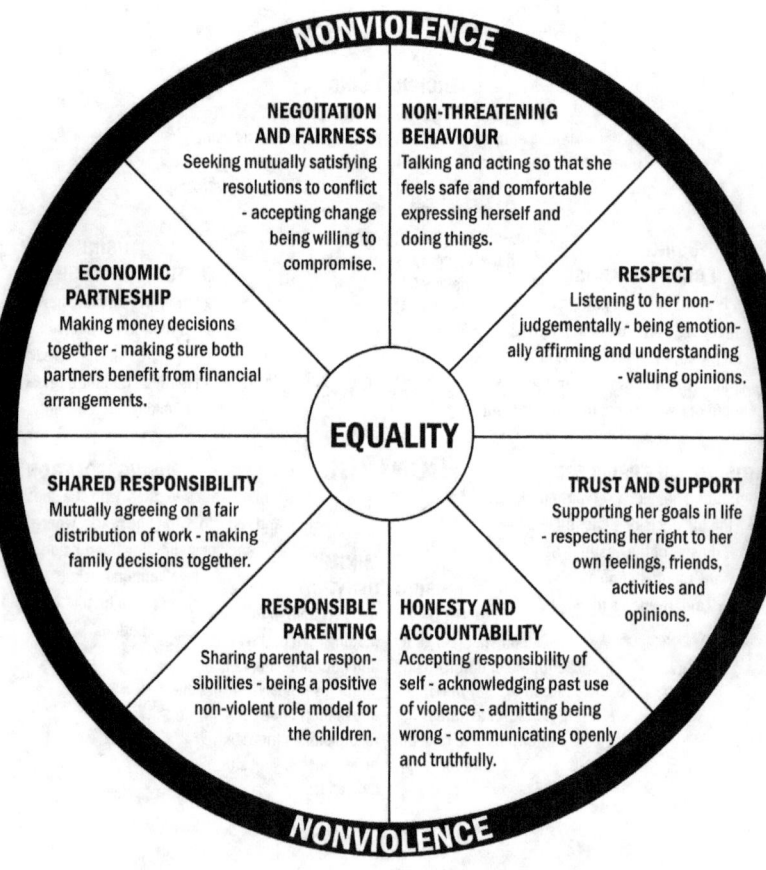

Figure from: www.theduluthmodel.org

Stopping the cycle of violence

You are an expert of your own life, even if you don't feel that way right now. If you are feeling numb, you may have shut down some feelings to cope with the violence. You know what makes you happy and what makes you sad, even if you are feeling numb and disassociated from the violence or if it has been going on for so long it just feels normal to you.

This chapter will acknowledge what you may be feeling, thinking and facing about your current position and the consequences of leaving your FDV relationship. It will provide you with information about available options, as well as explaining why setting boundaries legally using the police and court systems may be imperative.

The following *Chapter 7 Your Legal Rights* will give you the guidance on how to step forward and establish boundaries that you may need to ascertain for your safety both mentally and physically.

Your happiness counts

Self-care is a lifestyle and not an activity. Developing an effective self-care action plan of awareness, balance and connection will help you move forward. Awareness helps you recognise early warning signs. This awareness allows you to bring goals and strategies into your life to keep the different aspects of it in balance and maintain a connection with community (including social support) and family.

Being able to establish who drains your energy when you feel at your lowest is an important part of the process of starting self-care. Imagine you are like a bucket of water, your reservoir of what fills up your life. Who shoots holes in your bucket, draining away energy as you are constantly trying to refill the bucket? The *Cycle of Violence* will make victims feel extremely drained.

Ways that you can fill up your bucket:

- Positive self-talk
- Positive comments & encouragement from others
- An environment that brings you joy, such as a beach, park or walking track
- Unconditional love
- Awareness of strengths
- A positive self image
- Your good values and beliefs
- Self-reassurance

STOPPING THE CYCLE OF VIOLENCE

> **Things that empty your bucket:**
>
> - Negative self-talk
> - Isolation
> - Loneliness
> - Children's needs and wants
> - Ill health
> - Financial stress
> - Focusing on weaknesses
> - Disrespectful behaviour towards you
> - Negative comments from others
> - Being the target of violent and controlling behaviours

Constant put-downs retrain your brain and belief systems. Our subconscious brain absorbs information, whether it is true or not. It just absorbs the information. When you are being told repeatedly, your belief systems get rewired to believe the new information. Being with an abuser even for a short period can start rewiring your belief systems and can have you feeling down-hearted in no time. The opposite is also true, where positive beliefs are formed by the repetition of positive information.

The late Louise Hay wrote *Heal Your Life*, which became a worldwide best seller, and was translated into many different languages. She writes how the mind creates illness in the body just from negative thoughts; her book provides counter affirmations to re-correct the negative thoughts and thereby heal your body's ailments. This book has had a massive impact to the many lives of people and is a testament to how your thought processes can be easily changed with positive affirmations and thoughts. You and only you have the power to choose what you think!

What is something negative that your abuser has said that you now believe? Have they been critical of you and the things you do? Do they call you names and put you down? Do they humiliate you in front of others? Have you now adopted these negative opinions as your beliefs?

In what ways have you become to feel negative about yourself?

- Being critical of yourself
- Loss of confidence and no longer feeling attractive – e.g. feeling fat or ugly
- Feeling unworthy of love and support
- Feeling unworthy of financial fulfilment
- Feeling unable to trust others

Is this what you believed about yourself prior to the relationship or have you slowly gone downhill? When we become aware of how our patterns of relating have declined, we clearly see how we have become stuck in a cycle of trying to fix a relationship with someone we love. We see that we've romanticised the relationship, working towards the next honeymoon period without realising how much we have spiralled downwards. Just because you may have negative beliefs about your abilities right now, that does not mean it will stay that way. Nothing in this world stays the same, every cell of your body is replaced regularly and a new you can be recreated!

If you are caught up trying to fix your FDV relationship, your focus of happiness is external, not internal, which is why you may not be aware of the downward spiral you've endured. You may have been blind, because your ego mind is choosing the relationship above your needs for safety and security. When you are threatened and encounter the fight/flight/freeze reflex, you become abundantly aware of the internal battle to feel safe and the need for the externalised love. Confusion reigns, and then when the abuser offers to never re-offend, you accept this as truth and neglect the safety and security you desperately require.

You deserve respect for your needs, wants and desires for your own life. You are entitled to feel safe whilst you express how you feel to a loved one. Expressing yourself should not mean risking another round of the *Cycle of Violence*. If you cannot communicate your feelings without escalation, you need to ascertain whether you are really relating to the other person. A relationship should have open communication and acceptance of differences, and partners should be able to relate to one another's needs and wants. Everything in your relationship should be negotiable, so that both partners agree with outcomes, and one doesn't dominate or control the other.

Ego -vs- Self

Stay aware of where you are operating from. Are you being directed by your ego mind or your inner soul self? The inner self shall guide you from a loving place whereas the ego mind will justify its actions. Watch yourself operate. Where are you responding from? Where is your abuser operating from? Decide which mode of response is appropriate for the time/situation. You always have the choice.

If you are in *Ego* mode – choose to look at it from the *Self*, even if you start to respond from the ego. Understand your ego is trying to survive based on your programmed subconscious beliefs. The ego will keep you from your true self and make you feel separate from it. Know that the ego is a false self and it serves little purpose when trying to move beyond your hurt and pain. It is from the true self that you can grow and move forward. Understand that what you see in others as a problem is often a disowned part of your ego trying to self-protect, resisting change and therefore not really looking at the problem. For example, if you are over-loving an abusive partner, then you don't feel loved yourself. The ego mind will give you a reason to excuse their behaviour, as you are also feeling the same pain, but you mask it by over extending exactly what you need… to be loved, made secure and to be treasured. Your ego mind will convince you that through giving more, you will receive more. This is a false perception: your ego mind will convince you that you can change them to give you the love you need. This is not true. You need to give you the love you need to YOU. Look for solutions within. If you are having trouble understanding this process, my book *Mind Chatter That Matters* explains in detail how the ego mind seeks control and how you can learn to overcome the control and operate from your *true inner self*.

On the next page is a list of differences of the two:

STOPPING THE CYCLE OF VIOLENCE

Ego	Self
Want	Need
Fear	Love
Control	Allow
Selfishness	Self
Pain	Growth - Spiritual & Personal
Defence	Self-Protection
Aloneness/Separateness	Connected to Higher Power
Anger	Acceptance of Own Feelings
Demands	Communication
Assumptions	Truth
Judgement	Forgiveness

You will probably notice an abuser operates mainly from the ego because they are in pain. But during the honeymoon phase of the *Cycle of Violence* they appear to be operating from the *True Self*. Therefore it is confusing for victims, who feel the abuser is finally wanting and needing the healthy relationship. But as soon as conflict or tension reigns, they swing back over to the *Ego* and start the cycle again. This is like living in a make-believe relationship full of empty hope for the love and security we so desire.

Hurt people, hurt people

FDV relationships are much more difficult to leave than normal healthy relationships, but the effort is very much worth it. Survivors of FDV relationships always feel rewarded for exiting and setting boundaries. Being responsible for your own happiness and wellbeing, and the happiness and wellbeing of your children, must be your first priority. Acting to stop the cycle can be a daunting process, but this book will detail the steps.

Depending on the complexity of your situation and whether or not you have a clear head to be able to strategise your escape, you may need assistance in defining the stages you need to work through.

At the time you're trying to leave the relationship or withdraw emotionally, abuser's increase their control or manipulate to coerce you to stay. These are adapted behaviours to get their needs met, as they feel rejected, lonely, insecure and unloved. Remember, you have taught your abuser how to treat you and what works with you with your prior responses. They will persist to force you back into the position of which made them feel safe.

Setting new, firmer boundaries may incite another *Cycle of Violence*. It may be unlikely that you can calmly discuss your new boundaries if your partner is incapable of negotiating for the health of the relationship. However, some abusers seek help at this point and can recover, after significant assistance from trained professionals. The violence shall continue if the abuser does not take his own personal action and accept responsibility for the violence. If you make appointments for them, or try to fix them in other ways, you are taking the responsibility for fixing them.

Your attempts to fix your partner will be futile if they do not take responsibility or see that they have a problem. In our culture, women are not expected to express anger and if they do are labelled as crazy, psycho or a bitch. In contrast, is it generally more accepted for a man to get angry, possibly because it is believed this is the only way they can express their emotions. We all need the space to express who we are without doing the damage to the people we love and the relationships we wish to keep.

People who have been hurt and have not had the support to work through their issues, hurt others. They adapt their behaviours to get their needs met because they are in pain, but this should never be an excuse for them mistreating you. This is the reason that they should seek help. Professional help. If you are not professionally trained and are too close to the abuser, you cannot help other than to listen to their issues and guide them into getting the professional help they need. You can't force them to see their inappropriate coping methods or behaviours if they don't want to see them!

Everyone has hurt, it is part of human life. But when hurt is experienced, expressed appropriately and accepted, you can move on in life. This is preferable to responding with defensiveness and control in order to avoid the pain again. Abusers are often hurt people hurting others. But your love will not fix their hurt, regardless how much you give, show or tell.

Guide your partner to seek the help they need. You know how hard it is to change yourself and how it takes months of awareness before you understand why you do what you do and what you need to change. Changing yourself is hard enough. Imagine how much effort you need to make to change someone else, especially if they aren't prepared to look within and see what they need to change to be happier. You don't have that power to change another. STAY FOCUSED ON YOURSELF!

There are a lot of resources in the community for the perpetrators of violence. Some Australian States even have support centres/accommodation for men to assist them in seeking the help they need to stop the violence and start to relate to others healthily. Not-for-profit community organisations offer several different support services for the perpetrator and the victim as well as family support.

High risk indicators

Establishing the urgency to escape your relationship may be difficult, especially when you consider all the things you need to do to exit the relationship. Seeking further advice from trained professionals will help you establish the level of urgency and assess the complexity of your situation. Be totally honest with yourself and responsible for your own and your children's physical and psychological safety AT ALL TIMES! Does your abuser exhibit these indicators?

- Homicidal fantasies, threatens to kill or you believe they could kill you, your children, or your pets.
- Threatened or attempted suicide.
- Assault (including assault using a weapon), rape, sexual assault or choking, strangling or causing loss of consciousness.

- Threatens to harm your home, possessions, children, pets or other people you love.

- Stalking you or has extreme jealousy or possessiveness.

- Has breached a restraining order.

- Has abused under the influence of alcohol or drugs.

- Has a prior mental health diagnosis.

- Abuses you while you are pregnant.

- History of prior violence.

- Is aware you have plans to leave or are recently separated.

- Has been denied custody or access to the children.

Support network

You also may feel isolated from friends, family or other loved ones because of your relationship. Reconnect with them. Allow them to apologise for their lack of awareness for you have been through. Seek support from people who will not be judgemental, but instead supportive of your process.

- What safety nets can you put in place for support?

- Do you have people that support you emotionally? If so, who?

- Do you have safety for your kids, both physically and emotionally? Does their schooling provide support or extended family/friends?

- Who do you know who can help you with legal advice without cost to you?

- Who can you express all your emotions to without judgement?

- Who can help you financially if need be?

At this stage you may be experiencing heightened fear levels and should seek the services of a professional or a community centre that assists FDV clients and their families. You can be helped to work through your fear so that it doesn't hold you back or cause you to return to the violence.

Getting assistance to work through your step-by-step plan will help you throughout the planning process. A strategic plan is where you make each step into workable bits, put the bits in order and then work though a timetable of each step.

I highly recommend that you seek a professionally trained psychologist. Reach out to a trained professional if you do not think you can manage the process alone. Do not be afraid that this will be used against you.

In Australia, Medicare will provide you with 10 subsidised appointments for a psychologist on a *Mental Health Care Plan*. Go to your doctor and request one! When making the appointment for the psychologist you must ensure that they are willing to have their records or notes from your appointments subpoenaed to court. This is imperative!!! For the purposes of the Local Courts and Family Court of Australia, you need the records of a university-trained professional to prove your abuse. DO NOT SKIP THIS STEP! I will explain how fundamentally important it is in the next chapter.

STOPPING THE CYCLE OF VIOLENCE

Safety Planning

To accomplish each goal of escaping the relationship, you will need a step-by-step plan so that you do not feel overwhelmed by everything you need to manage.

You can download this *Safety Plan* at https://getoutgetfree.com/gogfdownloads or use the following pages here to list what you need to plan for.

My Personalised Escape Plan		
Police:	000 (Emergencies)	24 hours, 7 days a week
	131 444 (General Enquiries)	
Domestic Violence Hotline	1800RESPECT (1800 737 732)	24 hours, 7 days a week
Lifeline	131 114	
Local Shelter	Ph:_____	__ hours, __ days a week
Local Motel	Ph:_____	__ hours, __ days a week

a.	Find four people who I trust to tell about the abuse and might help me if I leave. My safe people are:
b.	Open a bank account in my name only and store the relevant information with a safe person.
c.	_____(who) will keep a bag for me and keep a spare mobile on charge for me or store some change for phone calls. I shall make sure I have all my contacts in my spare phone and keep some small change on me at all times or get a phone card.

GET OUT GET FREE

d.	_____(who) might be able to lend me money or have some saved in an account unknown by my abuser, so I can maintain my independence.
e.	_____(who) will take care of my pets for emergency care until I contact the RSPCA.

f.	Items to take or leave with a safe person (Copy documents if your abuser checks these are still located in the home):
	
	• Children (if safe)
	• Money/EFTPOS/Credit Card
	• Driver's licence
	• Keys to car/home/work
	• Extra clothes
	• Medical records
	• Medications/Prescriptions
	• Pensions/Health Care Card
	• School records
	• Immigrant information
	• Mobile phone with contact numbers
	• Items of sentimental value
	• Photos
	• Important paperwork including
	   • Prior restraining orders
	   • Birth certificates
	   • Passport
	   • Other ID
	   • Other licences
	   • Car registration
	   • Vaccination record
	   • Mortgage or lease agreement
	   • Insurance papers
	   • Parenting Plan (Contact orders)
	   • Divorce papers
	   • Marriage certificate

STOPPING THE CYCLE OF VIOLENCE

g.	Learn where to lead my abuser near a room with more than one exit such as a lounge room. Avoid rooms that are small and one door exit and any rooms that have weapons, such as kitchens and garages. Try to use going outside as an excuse to exit the house like taking out the rubbish, going to the shop or walking the dog.
h.	I will teach my children how to leave and where to hide safely and a code word for them to leave a get help from my safe people. I will tell them where stay safe and with whom. If they aren't available, I will give them another few options and teach them how to make a 000 call to the police.
i.	If I decide to leave, I will: (Method of leaving and practice how to get out safely. What doors, windows or exits will you use?).
j.	If I need to leave quickly I can leave my purse/wallet/keys on/in: (Leave these near an exit so that I can grab and run or hide them in a safe place outside or with someone safe)
k.	I can tell: about the violence and ask them to call the police if anything suspicious, angry or violent noises is heard from my home, a telephone call from me or my children. If they are not available I will also tell: about the violence so they can be my second/third fall back person.
l.	I will use a code word of _____ with my friends and children so they can call for help when I use it. (Prepare everyone with this).

GET OUT GET FREE

m.	If I have to leave my home, I will go to: (Make sure you have this plan in place even if you don't think you may need it). If I can't safely go to this place, I will go: I will try to do things that get me out of the house, such as empty the bins, walking the pet or going to the shop as a way of leaving.
n.	If I am expecting things to escalate into an argument, I will try to move the argument close to my exit plan in step (g).
o.	I will use my intuition if the argument is very serious and can give my abuser what they want to calm them down as I must protect myself until I/we am out of danger.
p.	I will change the stores I use to visit with my abuser so that they cannot stalk, harass me or abuse me.
q.	I will always carry my restraining order on me at all times.
r.	I will provide the schools, teachers and babysitters a copy of the restraining orders and any Parenting Plan from the Family Court.
s.	I will review my safety plan regularly and a friend has agreed to help me review this plan.
t.	When I feel down, tired and overwhelmed and ready to return to the abuser, I can:
v.	When I have to talk to the abuser, I can:

STOPPING THE CYCLE OF VIOLENCE

v.	I can do positive self-talk and tell myself : _____
w.	I can call _____ to help support me.
x.	There are other things that make me feel stronger than returning to my abuser _____
y.	I can attend support groups for Family Domestic Violence at _____ to gain strength and regain my confidence.

Solutions to consequences of staying or leaving

This section is to give you the knowledge and power to leave your relationship. Understanding the dynamics of your relationship is where you gain the motivation to change. Seeing how you have spiralled, deciding about your safety and wellbeing, planning the steps to exit the relationship or escape from your abuser, establishing boundaries and moving forward will give you the power to make choices for your future's happiness.

If this has been your first experience of abuse, and hopefully so, not all these plans, options and perceptions in this book will be appropriate to you, but it will still provide the avenues you need to think about and the processes of ending a relationship.

Weighing up the risks and consequences of staying or leaving the relationship can overwhelm you. Your mental wellbeing, strength and support will be major factors in when you chose to leave. The table on the following pages will give you options comparing "If I stay" and "If I leave", to help you think outside the restraint and concerns you are facing.

GET OUT GET FREE

	If I stay	If I leave
Physical	Continued hitting or injury Continued threats or actual death Damage to property Children witness more violence Children may be targeted or be hurt protecting me	Escalation of the violence Increases chances of you or the children being killed Damage to property Children may be targeted or hurt protecting me Increases risk of abuse during contact (visitation) Can't stop abuser regardless of restraining order
Financial	Limited money allocation Abuser could put bills in my name Abuser could quit or lose their job Might make me give up my job cont'd....	Might have to move out of family home Living on less money as a single parent Child support may be slow arriving, or your partner may avoid paying cont'd...

STOPPING THE CYCLE OF VIOLENCE

	If I stay	If I leave
Financial cont'd	Could be evicted due to damage Tied to a mortgage or loan Destroy things of importance	Unable to make loan repayments, which negatively affects your credit rating Might have to quit job to take care of children Might threaten your employment by creating drama Things of importance destroyed Might have to go into hiding, move the children to new schools, leave town and leave things behind in a rush Not have enough income to go to court to set boundaries and parenting orders for visitation No access to phone or technology

	If I stay	If I leave
	Verbal & physical abuse will continue	May continue abuse through access (visitation) for the children
	Mental health decline	Might use drugs or alcohol to cope with past and present problems
	Become reliant on drugs or alcohol to cope	Have family and friends threatened for helping you escape
	Lose support of family and friends if you don't leave	Might not have the support from family or friends if they don't want you to leave
	Family and friends may be victims of abuser	Suicidal thoughts or committing suicide
Psychological	Suicidal thought or commit suicide - both abuser and victim	May have language difficulties
		May have cultural challenges with support personnel or your family (e.g. when family members find out about the report of abuse)
		Might be deported
		Dishonour to my family or culture

Working through fears to exit your relationship

A well-known acronym is FEAR: "False Evidence Appearing Real" or "F@$k Everything And Run." We either face fear head on or use it as a reason to stall our progress.

When you think about fear, you realise it is actually projected thoughts about what may occur if you choose a path forward. Your ego mind is projecting the possibilities of what negative consequences may happen to prevent you from taking that path. The ego mind would prefer to stay with the security of what it knows rather than push through for the happiness you deserve.

A method of overcoming fearful thoughts is to find alternatives for each fearful projection your mind delivers as justification for staying put. Instead of giving in to the fearful thought, you can explore other options or gain further information in order to make alternative choices.

When you think about all the times you have moved through fear, you will have evidence of how you have overcome fearful thoughts. For example, when you learnt to drive and learnt how to drive a car, motorbike or even a truck. Or when you had to go for your first interview and start your first job. Or your first kiss. Your ego mind will keep placing fear in your path to prevent growth. You conquer fear by wanting and needing more than your fearful thoughts.

Once you have listed all the possible fearful consequences that may occur, you now need to establish alternative decisions you can make if the fear does become your reality. Tackle each fearful consequence one at a time, as this helps prevent you from being overloaded with endless mind chatter, holding you at ransom and from escaping the abuse.

You need to think outside the square, however. Below are some suggestions of ways to solve your fearful thoughts with other options you may not have thought of:

Escalation of the violence

- If you are confronted by the abuser, make sure you show empathy and respect, and apologise without accepting blame. Allow them to talk without interruption and respond quietly and calmly. Adopt a passive and neutral stance, minimise eye contact and where possible obey instructions so it isn't threatening to the abuser. Try to calm their threatening behaviour by acknowledging their issues. Keep a good distance between you and them, using furniture or a vehicle as a barrier until you can diffuse the situation or escape safely.

- You have the right to call 000 for help! You do not need to pay for this call, even if on a mobile phone without credit. Do not hesitate to call the police for protection. Even if you have been threatened with further violence, if you involve the police they will act to protect you, but you must be explicit about the level of violence (including the use of weapons), so they know how urgent your case is. Under no circumstances should you allow a police officer to dismiss the level of violence you are experiencing, nor take your claims of violence as superficial. You must demand the level of protection you want! If the police have been called numerous times by you or your children, you must insist on the protection you need. In certain circumstances it might be safer to wait for your abuser to calm down and plan your escape when they are not

STOPPING THE CYCLE OF VIOLENCE

present. Other cases you may be too frightened to obtain a restraining order. In some state the police may obtain a restraining order automatically without your consent.

- When the police are involved or are called out to attend to you, try to stay as calm as possible as often under stress you can emotionally escalate, often with aggression. The police can get confused if your abuser is calm and your are explosive due to the level of abuse. Be assertive, even when emotional!

- If there are children involved in the violence the police will make a report to your State's Children's Protection Department as part of attending the call.

- Ensure that you get the attending police officer's contact name and number as well as an event/report number from the police officer. This may be required later for court and you will need this number as well as their details.

- There are also specialised FDV units within the police force, so ask more about what will be reported and who to contact.

- Consider getting a restraining order for the longest period possible. In some States the police will do this on your behalf automatically, in other States you will need to ask for one or apply directly to the Local Court yourself. This is imperative if you wish to get support through Centrelink and other government departments as proof that you are in hardship and suffering from FDV. Please see *Chapter 7 Your Legal Rights* to refer to the impact on you when making an application for *Parenting Orders* (contact or visitation orders on how you parent or co-parent) when you do not have a restraining order. Restraining orders are not a charge on the abuser. However, when the abuser breaches a restraining order, then they are charged with a criminal offence.

- Call 1800RESPECT or find a local community service provider that has FDV services. These numbers should be on your *Safety Plan* as detailed on page 109.

- Escape the environment until things cool down and go to a safe place where the abuser won't find you, such as you might go to the home of a friend or family member, a refuge, a motel, or a rental property.

- If your abuser refuses to accept the restraining order and asks for a court hearing, go to the hearing and take any evidence you have about why you need the restraining order. Keeping records of abuse is imperative, as well as police event/report numbers to substantiate the calls and events. Make sure you get a psychologist's report for the hearing detailing any psychological threats or abuse you may have encountered. Keep in mind an abuser often abuses behind closed doors. Ammunition such as reports from medical professionals can be used in court to substantiate your case of abuse and the need for protection.

- Notify a good neighbour to call the police if they hear anything or see if they can be a safe place for children to run to.

Increased chances of you or the children being killed

- CARRY A COPY OF YOUR RESTRAINING ORDER ON YOU AT ALL TIMES.

- If you are in fear of your lives, you need a restraining order without hesitation. There are refuges for women to escape to. Unfortunately, there are currently no refuges for men escaping violence.

- Refuges cannot turn you away even if they lack the accommodation for you and your children. They will fund accommodation overnight in a hotel or motel for your safety as part of a crisis plan. Ask about the intake process, age/gender eligibility, disability access if needed and the maximum number of family members they can take in. Make sure that you rehearse a plan so that you are more comfortable when the time comes. This means visiting the refuge, so you know who will help you and where you might end up so that you know in advance what you might be facing. Removing the unknown by seeing where you can protect yourself and your children will ease some of your fear. Keep in mind that some refuges will not take male children over a certain age for the safety of the other children. This means you will need to find a plan to accommodate your boy/s when they exceed this age limit. As part of your safety plan, make it a priority to check with your refuge for the age limit. Do they have a friend or family member the abuser doesn't know who could look after them in the short-term?

- Once you have a restraining order in place, you can make an application to the Family Court for *Parenting Orders*. You should do this whilst the restraining order is current. Please see below and in *Chapter 7 Your Legal Rights* how your Local Court can make changes to parenting orders. Ask for supervised contact for your children so that abuser has contact only whilst under supervision by a community organisation. This gives the abuser the ability to still maintain their relationship with their children, and safeguards the children during the contact. The court will receive reports about the amount of contact and the quality of it, as well as of the abuser's behaviour during the supervised contact. It will use the reports when making future parenting orders.

- If there are <u>no</u> Family Court parenting orders in place, the other parent has equal and shared custody of the children and can take the children from school, from your front yard or from you whilst shopping. There is nothing stopping them as they have joint custody. This is why, when a restraining order is placed, you must ask that your children are included in the order. If you cannot get them included, they are at risk of being taken by the abuser and there is nothing you can do about it because of the joint custody. The police will not do anything because there are no Family Court parenting orders in place. Make sure you advise their school of your situation so that they advise you if your children are removed during school. Get straight to Family Court once you have your restraining order and make an application, even without the legal representation if you can't afford it. These applications are simple to make. If you make an urgent order because of the FDV and the restraining order, the Family Court will act fairly quickly to have a parenting order made for your children, at least temporarily.

- If there are Family Court parenting orders in place, the other parent is restricted to certain contact. When you apply for a restraining order at the Local Court, you must ask the magistrate to make modifications to the Family Court parenting orders as a temporary order. Under the *Family Court Act Section 68R*, a Local Court has the power to make this change to the order to prevent a child being exposed to child abuse of any kind and to protect the family from further FDV. However some Local Courts may only make these changes in regional areas but they are not restricted to those areas as city victims can apply to Family Court immediately to have their parenting orders modified. There is a limited time frame during which the Local Court can make this change, and the abuser may use tactics to change the hearing to another court location to extend the hearing date beyond that time frame. Abusers will often say that you are using a restraining order to alienate them from their children, therefore some magistrates are reluctant to make these changes to a federal court order. If you have Family Court proceedings in place, the magistrate may not be willing to make the necessary changes to the Family Court parenting orders. You must insist on this change for the protection of yourself and your children.

- Ensure that you notify the school or child care centre of the restraining order and provide them with a copy, along with instructions of what they must do should your abuser breach the orders.

- Pack an overnight bag and keep it somewhere safe. Make sure that your abuser won't discover missing items. Consider putting your important documents in this bag including extra prescriptions, spare credit card and any financial documents you may need. Keep a spare house and car key if you can. Give all these to your safe person for safe keeping, or leave a set hidden in the garden. Refer to the *Safety Plan* on page

109 for a list of documents.

- Keep your keys handy all the time and make sure that if you're planning to leave in your car, that the car is parked with easy access to drive away.

- Consider your transport options if you don't have a car or can't get access to it. Do you have enough money for a taxi or uber, can you call family or friends, are you close to public transport with a timetable?

- Make sure your mobile phone is charged regularly, is handy, and speed dials are set for the emergency contacts you have.

- Teach your children to memorise the '000' police number, your phone number and address or how to make a reverse charge phone call. Rehearse where they can go to stay safe if the violence escalates or where to go to and call the safe person. Make sure they will be going to responsible adults who also know your plan if the children do arrive on their doorstep or meet them somewhere.

Damage to property

- If the abuser is damaging your property and they are not living in the house or have been removed from your property, ensure you are insured for unlawful damage in your own name. If their name is on the insurance, some insurance companies will not pay out for damages.

- Keep your precious valuables and keepsakes in a place that you can grab and flee with them easily if possible or remove them to safe keeping prior to escaping without the abuser knowing they are missing.

- If they are threatening to burn the house down, make sure your smoke alarms are in good working order with regular battery testing and changes.

- If they are stalking you from outside, ensure you have your blinds closed so that they cannot see you and what you are doing in the house. Call the police and take photos if possible.

- If stalking from a distance, such as work or shopping centre, take photos of them.

Children may be targeted or hurt protecting me

- A restraining order is a dire need if your children are being physically abused. You must protect them and remove them from the abuser. Call the police on 000 without hesitation.

- Remove the child from the environment as safely as possible.

- Have your child/ren stay at a friend's house for a sleepover when the tension is building to the *explosive* phase if possible.

Increased risk of abuse during contact (visitation)

- Organise a contact changeover with a different person or organisation. Contact changeover is provided by different service providers within each state of Australia.

- It is very difficult to prove the abuser is putting your child at further risk at unsupervised contact. You need proof of the abuse. This is a precarious problem that many victims have in protecting their children. Without a restraining order, your hands will be tied to protect the children. In particular if you are not close to a Family Court, as in you are in a regional area, with a restraining order, you can have the Family Court's parenting orders modified by the Local Court for a short term until you make an application to the Family Court for the change in parenting orders or apply for new parenting orders.

- If your child is at further risk of physical and psychological abuse and is too scared to tell the Police for fear of their own life or threats to your life, you need to request in writing (e.g. email) medical and psychological assistance for the child, particularly if they are exhibiting the behaviours as outlined in *Chapter 4 FDV & its Impact*. YOU MUST NOT OMIT THIS REQUEST IN WRITING, even if they refuse to acknowledge the request, keep sending it in writing daily. You can make requests to the abuser via text message, so that you have proof that you are involving them in the decisions for the wellbeing of their child. Yes, it may seem like a ridiculous request to ask an abuser to have the child they are abusing tended to, however if you don't the Family Court will see that you are not involving the other parent (even if abusing the child) in the decisions that both parents must make. When you place this request in writing, you cannot be accused of obtaining the medical assistance for the child without the consent of the other parent. If you omit this request, then the evidence taken to court can be 'thrown out' as the other parent can claim that you are attempting to alienate them from the child and that the medical professional will have a biased view as they have not had to opportunity to have input to the child's wellbeing from both parents. If they

STOPPING THE CYCLE OF VIOLENCE

do not give their consent, the Family Court will probably see them in the light of neglecting the child's wellbeing. As if any abuser will consent to their behaviour being revealed and recorded by a medical professional to be used against them in court as evidence of the abuse! Make sure that you report all levels of abuse, including your own, to your doctor and that they document all events. Ask them to do this on both your record and your child's. Ask the doctor to create a *Mental Health Care Plan* for your child and place a referral to a psychologist or child psychiatrist. Getting the assessment of a university-trained professional will give you evidence that the court cannot dismiss.

- Every time your child reports any form of abuse, contact your State's Child Protection Department and make a report, regardless of how minute the neglect may be. Not feeding your child the right foods, ignoring their health issues, failing to ensure schooling attendance or completion of homework all constitute as neglect. If medical assistance is required, seek a regular doctor for the report or go to the emergency department of your closest hospital.

- If your child returns from a visitation with bruises, photograph them immediately. Ask the child to tell you how the bruises occurred and record your child via video or voice recording without them knowing you are doing it, so that it can be used in court to protect your child. If you advise your child you are recording, then this evidence may not be used in court.

- If a child is extremely distressed and cannot deal with contact with the abuser, seek urgent medical assistance from your doctor and ask for a *Section 1A* medical report. This is a psychological assessment made without a person's consent. It normally involves three different psychiatry specialists' opinions on the mental state of the child. If the child is suffering from acute stress or another associated condition, the specialist will report this back to your doctor. The specialists all report the abuse to your State's Child Protection Department. You also can report this to the department and they will often advise for the child to not have contact with the abuser. This is a fundamental process that you may need to follow through with if your child is distressed. The Family Court will take this report seriously when making parenting orders for the child.

Can't stop abuser regardless of restraining order

- Contact the police when a restraining order is breached so that the evidence is recorded, regardless of the level of the breach.

- Demand that the police act on the minor issues and have your abuser charged for the breach of the restraining order. Do not let them dismiss you because they have more important levels of concerns to deal with. Hopefully your abuser will get the message that the restraining order is in place for a reason and that they must follow the law or receive consequences for their breach of order.

- Take photographs of the abuser if they are stalking or harassing you.

- Record the abuser but make sure you include you saying on

the recording: "I am recording you….", so that you can take the evidence into Civl Court. Once they continue they have acknowledged that they are being recorded and then it is no longer a breach of their privacy and the recording can be used in court for a breach of restraining order.

- Refuse to respond to any breach of the restraining order, including text messages, phone calls, emails, knocks at the door or other requests for contact. The more you respond, the more the abuser will attempt to control you and your decisions. Keep records of everything. Don't just leave emails on your computer, print them out and store them in a safe place. Print out screen shots of your text messages and call log for proof of breach to support your claims in court.

Might have to move out of family home

- Whether you stay in your home or move to other accommodation, consider installing sensor lights, a peep hole and safety chain on your door and changing the locks.

- If you have a restraining order and remain in a rented home, seek tenancy support. Many States throughout Australia now support tenancy for FDV victims, whereby you can make changes to a lease for a property you rent, including being removed from a lease and getting your bond returned to you.

- If you jointly own a home with your abuser that has a mortgage over it and you have a restraining order, consider contacting the lending institution to see if you can extend your repayments. Many lenders are willing to give you some leeway under these circumstances.

- Often an abuser will leave you with a lot of financial debt to control you or punish you. Think of ways of getting financial assistance such as Centrelink. If you are under an income limit you will be entitled to a Health Care Card, which reduces some costs for medical needs, prescriptions, travel, entry to events, licences and licensing a motor vehicle. Centrelink will recognise FDV when you have a restraining order and you can request a hardship grant and urgent payment so that you have immediate funds to help assist you financially. Ensure that you persist with Centrelink, as the support you get can make a world of difference to your pocket, sense of independence and freedom. Currently the Commonwealth Bank offers $1000 to customers who have had a savings account with them for 6 months or more to help financially to escape FDV.

- If you are not a resident of Australia, contact Centrelink and apply for a *Exceptional Circumstances* payment. This payment is the equivalent to their Newstart payment. You will need a restraining order or Police intervention to obtain this.

- Make sure you have investigated the availability of safe places you could move to in a hurry, such as a refuge (as described above), the home of a family member, a friend's house, a hotel, a motel or a new rental home.

- Ensure that you have enough money put aside or saved in a safe place unbeknown to your abuser, so that you can escape if need be. Make sure you have enough for a few days' needs at a minimum.

- Make sure there are a few toys, clothes and any items that make your children feel secure stored with some friends.

Children settle quicker when they have some possessions of their own.

- Ensure you have certified copies of all your important documents. Certified is when you copy your document and have a Justice of the Peace sign the printed copy that it is a copy of the original document. Keep these with someone safe outside of your home. Documents such as Medicare Cards, Drivers Licence, Motor Vehicle Registration/Licence, bank statements, birth certificates, marriage certificates, passports, and pet registrations should be copied. Remember to get some photos too.

- The housing departments of most States have bond assistance loans or may pay the full amount to help you get out of your home safely. They assist with funding the bond and also a few weeks rent, but check your State's department as it varies within each state. Emergency housing still has wait lists and getting it can still take months.

Living on less money as a single parent

- There are ways to minimise expenses and if you are in financial difficulty, swallow your pride and ask for help. It is much better when you feel you have the support of others.

- If you have nothing except the clothes on your back, then go directly to a charity or ask a friend to post on social media for donations. You will be surprised at the assistance you get. There are specific charities and refuges that give items away to assist victims of FDV.

- If you qualify, apply for a Centrelink Health Care Card. With this, most utility supply companies will give you a concession on the supply of gas, phone, electricity, water etc. Check with the relative companies for discount information.

- Some States have financial assistance for low income earners when bills exceed a certain value. Check with your FDV support person for the funding in your State.

- Most charities can assist with funding for petrol, food and amenities. Don't be afraid to ask, they are more than happy to help – helping people like you is often exactly the reason the charity began. Charities also provide cooked meals for the homeless and unfortunate, go have a good meal if you can't feed your family.

- Minimise the housing you need and make changes to your budget.

- There are financial counsellors in the charity and not-for-profit sector who will assist you when lenders, utility companies or credit providers are pressuring you and will help negotiate repayments on your behalf. They also help you develop and follow a budget.

- Revisit your income requirements, possibly taking on employment or reducing the time you spend working to get the work-life-money balance.

- Organise with family or friends to help you out temporarily. Most Australians are happy to help people in crisis. Don't be too embarrassed to ask for help.

- Find childcare in your area. Centrelink recipients receive heavily discounted rebates.

- In some circumstances you can get early access to your superannuation when in dire circumstances.

- Go to your local government (council) for the support services within your community. They have resources and specific listings for community service providers you can contact for funding to assist your move. They will also have contact details for FDV support groups. Going to one of these will make you feel less stressed and insane.

- Should you have pets and are terrified of moving and leaving them behind, the RSPCA has emergency accommodation for pets involved in FDV. Call them to obtain their support. They are very helpful and will accommodate farm animals, domestic animals and even birds!

Child support may be slow arriving or your partner may avoid paying

- The Child Support dilemma is a cumbersome process to say the least. You can go on their website to do an estimate of what your payments will be. Keep in mind that if your ex doesn't want to pay on a regular basis, you may have to wait up to six months for your first payment once they locate your ex-partner's employment or tax return refund. Often ex-partners feel the money is going directly to you, but looking after children is an expensive venture. Some ex-partners leave their jobs, so they don't have to pay you anything other than the minimal rate. Other ex-partners leave their jobs every time Child Support starts to deduct their wages for the payments due to you. Be prepared for a mine field of issues, and lack of clarity about when your payments may come through.

Treat them like a bonus when they do arrive. Many abusers use the child support payments as another way to control and punish you. They claim to the court system they are fantastic parents, whilst not meeting their financial obligations to support their children. Abusers must be willing to support their children, not punish them for choosing loyalties. Child Support tries to make the collection of your payments as easy as possible, but they are restrained as to what they can do and need to follow the guidelines strictly. Be prepared for ludicrous claims from your ex, such as you are doing cash work, avoiding taxes, working when you are not, or living a luxurious lifestyle. Your ex-partner may under estimate what they really earn to pay less, earn undeclared income or cash or reduce their earnings to pay you less child support. The calculations for child support can be done pre or post tax assessment, which makes it messy to reconcile and budget to. Ex-partners can accrue thousands of dollars and keep dodging the system. Sometimes you may need to wait years for payments or you may stay on their books forever. It is the luck of the draw of how your ex-partner wants to play the game, whether they want to pay you or punish you, how well they know the system and how manipulative they are.

Unable to make loan repayments and credit rating destroyed

- Call your lender and explain your situation. Ask for time to sort through your finances, mortgage and living expenses.

- If you are claiming a payment from Centrelink, you may be eligible for an advance. Contact them for more details.

- Facing bankruptcy because of your situation is daunting and soul destroying. However, over time, you become a statistic, a number in a book of many others, and declaring yourself bankrupt reduces a massive amount of stress, releasing the pressure so you can start again. It takes 3 years to be discharged from bankruptcy, and your credit rating for future borrowing will be affected for 5 years. Bankruptcy means your ability to travel overseas is affected, you'll be released from unsecured loans, you may lose your home or vehicle depending on value and the lender's security of the loan, and you'll be listed on a register. However, you are able to keep your goods and chattels if you declare bankruptcy. Depending on your earnings within the 3 years, you may be required to repay some of the debt.

- Make sure you remove your abuser from your utility bills, credit cards, insurance policies and bank accounts. Ensure you have enough funds to cover your costs.

- SEPARATE YOUR CASH IN YOUR BANK ACCOUNT PROMPTLY. Should your partner withdraw funds from a joint account whilst you're together, there is nothing you can do. However, if they withdraw after your separation, it becomes part of the settlement.

Might have to quit job to take care of children

- You can make an application for a Parenting Payment from Centrelink to assist you with living costs.

- It reduces your contribution to the calculation of child support percentage and your ex-partner may need to pay more, leaving you short if they don't.

- Look for an alternative position, work from home, change careers or work part time.

- Get a work-life balance if you can. Sometimes working under all the stress is better for you than being stuck at home with children and little money.

- Consider childcare for some days so that you can recharge. Centrelink has great subsidies for single parents who want to work. Speak to a social worker at Centrelink to find out more options that might be available to you.

Might threaten your employment by creating drama

- It is not acceptable for your ex to turn up at your workplace. You may feel like your job is at risk due to their behaviour or recurring abuse.

- There are new Fair Work Australia laws that have come into effect that provide FDV victims with support and time away from work. Your workplace should have a *Safety Policy* in place. Nevertheless, even many government departments, local governments, large corporations and small businesses haven't yet figured out how to manage the new law, let alone ensure procedures are in place for safety of their employees.

- Advise your workplace that you are enduring FDV and ask for time off if needed. Make sure your employer is are aware of how violent your abuser may be and discuss strategies for calming the abuser or ensuring the safe exit of all concerned. Make sure the employer calls the police if needed. Let them sort through their responsibilities for you as an employer.

They are not allowed to disengage your employment due to FDV.

Destroy things of importance

- Be prepared if your abuser is destructive to your belongings. Remove the very important and sentimental items or hide them away.

- They may still destroy some of your belongings. However, if they are being violent, call the police. Behaviour such as this is an attempt to control you and your decisions.

Might have to go into hiding, move the children's schools, leave town and leave things behind in a rush

- Moving to a new area means schooling needs to be arranged for your children. Most schools will not expect you to pay fees when fleeing a situation of FDV. The school's Parents & Child committees (P&C) are very helpful in finding or funding uniforms for your children. Ask for donations of text books from the school or agree to repay any schooling costs over a period.

- Be aware that if you are moving schools without a restraining order, your abuser may claim you are alienating them and haven't asked permission to uplift the children to a new environment. The Family Court doesn't take too kindly to one parent making decisions without consulting the other. If you don't have a restraining order, anything you do with the children without the other's consent may be used against you in Family Court.

- If you leave your home quickly without your possessions, you can return to get some of your belongings with police protection.

You do not have enough income to go to court to set boundaries and parenting orders for visitation

- Make sure you make an enquiry to Legal Aid even if you do not want to use them! Once the enquiry is made by either partner, they can only represent the first enquirer. If your partner enquires with them, they cannot support you, even if your partner's income means he's ineligible. This is often a tactic used by abusers to prevent you from getting any free legal support. One legal body cannot represent both parties, as this is deemed to be a 'conflict of interest'.

- Legal Aid will not support you with regards to a property settlement but will support you with parenting orders.

- If you are having to apply to a Local Court for a restraining order, in some States the police will represent you, in others you must self-represent. It is an easy process. On Local Court days, the number of restraining orders issued can make you feel like sheep being pushed through mounting yards. Hundreds of these are handed out weekly. There are safe rooms for FDV victims so that you don't need to sit out in the waiting rooms waiting to be called. You should ask a court representative to help you return to your vehicle or have someone come with you to escort you home. Many abusers become violent after court hearings. Restraining Orders are just that, restraining the abuser from contacting you in the ways stipulated on the order. Make sure you cover every aspect of contact methods for the protection of both you and your children. Refer to the Family Court Act, Section 68R, which details how a local Local Court can make temporary changes to any parenting orders you may have. Demand the magistrate makes the changes so that you and your children are not exposed to further violence. Make an urgent application to the Family Court for revised orders. Once a restraining order is issued by the Local Court and it is breached, contact the police immediately with evidence of the breach. Occasionally, minimal breaches will result in warnings. Severe breaches end up with court dates and criminal charges. You must report every breach, as it stacks evidence against the abuser and the police will act to restrain the abuser. If you are being abused psychologically, ensure you tell the abuser you are recording them. You can then use this evidence in court for the breach. Alternatively, have a witness with you every time you need to have contact with the abuser or have a report from your psychologist of the abuse. You can subpoena the psychologist's notes as evidence. Document every breach in a daily diary and have your witness do the same thing. The diaries can be used in court as evidence. Use ink pen, not pencils in order for each entry to be legitimate. You must stay on top of the game with abusers. You may think it is exhausting, but getting relief from their abuse will give you back your energy and be free to move forward.

No access to phone or technology

- Abusers can damage the phones, computers and equipment or they remove it from your possession to prevent you from getting access to the support you may need.

- Telstra have a program to assist women victims of FDV, whereby they provide a free phone to assist victims get safe.

- You could purchase a cheap second mobile phone and put all your contacts in it, especially the ones that you need for immediate support, both professional and personal. Give this to a safe person and ask them to keep it charged ready for use.

- Make sure all the web browsing pages you visit are deleted from your history and create an easy to remember password for each of your accounts you log into.

- Don't allow or use automatic passwords and access on your web browser or mobile phone. Make sure you re-enter your passwords each time.

- Minimise location sharing on your mobile device and, if you have a Google account, make sure you sign out of it so that your abuser doesn't get access to your location. Turn off location services in your mobile phone's settings, as well as geo-tagging for photos. Manage applications that access your location and decline location access in any applications you may install in the future.

- Check your social media settings to prevent others seeing your details. Make your posts private or don't post at all for a while. Never share your location when posting. Never share details about your identity, life or location.

- If you are automatically logged into email, social media or other accounts on your mobile, always log out in the future. Change your passwords if you think your abuser may have access to your accounts. Where possible use a two-step factor log-in for your accounts.

- Run an anti-spyware application on your phone to ensure nobody can track your phone activity or use it as a listening device. Alternatively change to a safe phone.

May continue abuse through access (visitation) for the children

- Ask another friend or family member to do the contact/access/visitation changeover.

- Do the changeover at a police station or public place like McDonalds where there are CCTV cameras operating. Put in writing the request and if the abuser doesn't correspond to your request, document this for Family Court and demand the changeover location be changed/added in your parenting orders.

- Record any abuse that the children witness, even if it is a voice recording on your mobile phone in your pocket. This evidence can be used in Family Court to substantiate why you want changeover in a safe place. You do not need the abuser's consent for evidence when recording or providing evidence in the Family Court.

- If you have a restraining order, the Family Court will often request or comply to a request for supervised contact of your children for the abuser. Supervised contact is an environment that is often funded by the State Government or Charity to protect victims of FDV from further abuse. Demand that supervised visits are included as part of the parenting orders.

Might use drugs or alcohol to cope with past and present problems

- If you are addicted to illicit drugs or use an excessive use of alcohol, seek professional help. Using these stimulants will only give you a low after the high and may make you more susceptible to mental illness or not being able to cope with the stress and strains of leaving an FDV relationship. You know when you are abusing these stimulants. Do not ignore the warning signs.

- The same must be mentioned for prescription drugs: ensure you do not exceed the prescribed dose. If they are ineffective, consult your medical practitioner for a review.

- If you are not coping with the care of your children, money, cooking or maintaining a home, you need help. Swallow your pride and ask for help. You are not always going to be indestructible and self-sufficient. No one can cope with the onslaught and fall out of FDV alone. Everyone needs to reach out for support. Reaching out doesn't make you weak, it merely says that you are capable of fixing issues with the view of another person's experience, opinion or judgement, at a time when your stress levels may inhibit your problem-solving skills or your full thinking potential.

- If you have depression or anxiety from FDV, it is widely recognised that victims suffer these conditions. You may even be diagnosed with a mental illness. However, if you are being treated by a medical professional for the condition and taking the necessary medication prescribed, the Family Court will look at you as a responsible parent, taking care of yourself so that you can take care of the children.

- Should you be accused of taking illicit drugs or being an alcoholic, the Family Court has the children's best interest at heart, not yours. Ensure that you are stable and in a good place to take care of your children or you could lose your contact and the tables could be turned to allow the abuser to have the full contact. This is a devastating fact. So, maintain your responsibility to take good care of yourself so that you are the best possible parent to your children.

- Unravelling why you ended up in an FDV relationship is a healthy process and can be better understood with the help of a trained professional. Psychologists are trained to assist clients with FDV and often represent a long-term parental role model as to what you deserve in relationships. I couldn't recommend enough that you should seek the help you need. If you are not happy with a psychologist and the person doesn't seem like a good fit, change and find another. You must have a sense of safety and good rapport with your psychologist.

Have family and friends threatened for helping you escape

- Have your family and friends obtain a restraining order if the abuser persists.

- You are not responsible for how they respond to your abuser's behaviour.

- Ask them not to share your location in order to keep you safe.

- Tell them to call the police if necessary.

- Advise what you have instigated with restraining the abuser. Make sure you also advise them of the degree of violence you have experienced so they know what may happen to them.

Might not have the support from family or friends if they don't want you to leave

- If you have complained several times and done nothing, they may be feeling like you are 'the boy who cried wolf' and ignore your requests. You need to act to exit the relationship anyway, and get other help if family or friends have not offered or are avoiding it.

- Avoiding issues or putting your head in the sand isn't a resolution. You need to be strong for you and the children. Ask for help until family and friends understand your desperate need.

- Most people don't want to deal with drama, nor are they skilled to manage it. Sometimes they have been traumatised previously themselves or they don't want further issues with the abuser. Understand that not everyone can give you the assistance you need.

- You may have exhausted your avenues for financial assistance from family and friends and find they are not willing to continue to assist you.

- You need to respect how much someone is willing to give. Everyone has their limits. Be reasonable and appreciate the boundaries of what they are willing to give. Once you start taking serious action they may change their minds and assist you. Leave the door open and do not judge them. There are plenty of resources in the community to assist you if they are not willing. Don't make this an excuse to not seek the help you need.

Suicidal thoughts or commit suicide

- Should you, your child or the abuser threaten or attempt suicide SEEK PROFESSIONAL HELP IMMEDIATELY! Do not wait. Unless you are trained in suicide prevention you are not likely to be able to assist people at risk of suicide correctly.

- There are telephone lines that people can call to discuss how they are feeling and what steps to take. You can call these lines as well to get some advice on what to do next.

- Suicide is prevalent in society. These at-risk people are dealing with many facets of life they cannot cope with. Suicide seems the only solution to their pain.

- Should your abuser threaten suicide if you do not comply to their requests, still seek the help they need or refer them to the help. You cannot control another's choices, but you can intervene. The last thing your children need is for one of their parents to take their own life, regardless of the circumstances and levels of abuse. Children need a relationship with each parent. They can choose the level of contact they have as they get older, not you.

- The stress on child victims of FDV can often cause them to have suicidal thoughts or suicide attempts. Check in with your children to how they are feeling on a regular basis.

- Watch out for…withdrawal, moodiness, alcohol and/or drug

use, radical behaviour, putting others first, changes in their personality and giving away their personal possessions. Listen to…."I'm fine, leave me alone, nothing I can do, what do you care, I don't want to worry anyone, I'm just going away" statements. Pay attention to their feelings…. pain, worry, feelings of being overwhelmed or exhausted. They may be suffering controlled grief, trapped anger, hopelessness, loss of identity or expectation, and want to be with others who have already died. These symptoms can be contributing to suicidal thoughts or suicide attempts. If there are no clear answer, ask them "Have you made a plan to suicide?" Don't be afraid, as this can turn things around for them. You can keep them safe by staying with them until you get a professional involved who can assist them. Don't try to solve all their problems or give them reasons or solutions. Keep them safe from harming themselves. Do not promise secrecy, promise to be discerning and discreet. Do not miss, dismiss or avoid the issue, even if you don't know what to do. This can be a difficult issue to manage but you will be in a better head space than the person at risk. Suicide can be prevented. Help-seeking is encouraged by open, direct and honest talk about suicide. Get the telephone number for a crisis line and telephone them and introduce the person at risk and their situation. Then hand over the phone. Alternatively seek someone face to face. Remember TALK…Tell, Ask, Listen, KeepSafe.

May have language difficulties

- Most community service providers and government departments can provide an interpreter for anyone that is unable to communicate using the English language.

- Ask for one and they shall arrange it.
- Use the Google application on your phone call *Google Translate*. You can convert any language to English and vice versa.
- Seek brochures that are available in your language.

May have cultural challenges with support personnel or their families finding out about the report of abuse

- There is immense shame for reporting abuse within some cultures and it is expected that you keep the secret of the abuse. This is not accepted within the Australian law and you will be provided the protection you need.

- Some community service providers specialise in meeting the needs of Indigenous and Torres Strait Islanders where family groups have FDV present. Ensure your information is kept confidential. Some of these family groups may have family members who are the community service workers. Find another service if you are not comfortable and have fears that they may be sharing your information.

Might be deported or children taken

Many FDV victims that have not yet obtain residency status are terrified that they will be deported or lose their children. FDV victims are able to get support to obtain a different visa. Seek a support service that can help in this instance.

Dishonour to my family or culture

Unfortuneately some cultures have barbaric forms of punishment within their culture to control individuals and believe they have culture rights and obligations to uphold in order to sustain the cultures' survival. In Australia, you have rights as a human being to be an individual before your cultural rights. Cultural punishment is an intersecting factor that keeps FDV victims grid-locked into conforming to cultural rules rather than be banished from the culture altogether either by honor killings or exclusion. Honour killings are illegal in Australia and will be treated as murder regardless of cultural beliefs.

Support

Stress is a normal response to everyday life. Be aware when your stress levels have become elevated as it can be a health hazard.

During change, we need to cope with the differences and make adjustments to grow and become happier. Developing a coping plan will help you prepare yourself as you move through the stages of exiting your relationship. Remember you can make changes in your life. Notice tension and do things to reduce it, find a relaxation method and reach out when tension gets too high.

Reduce life's stresses by considering:

- Lifestyle changes – such as exercise, bush walking, sharing etc. Do one thing each day to improve your life.

- Notice tension in your body. Do meditation, deep breathing, muscle relaxation or use your imagination to uplift your mind and body.

- Catch unhelpful thoughts ("I can't cope", "I'm a terrible person" etc.) and try to think about what led you to feel the way you do. Make a decision to choose more realistic and helpful thoughts.
- Write a journal of the feelings you experience.
- Write down some coping statements and things you can do to help calm you down when stress erupts ("I can do it", "I've done this before", "I've just got to stick to my plan").

Your support from an external professional should entail:

- Helping you develop the discipline to follow through and giving you someone to be accountable to.
- Preventing you from feeling overwhelmed.
- Helping you check if the steps are real and adequate.
- Checking if there are any resources needed.
- Discussing or uncovering any obstacles.
- Managing your decisions going forward, after you reach your goal.

Rebuilding you

There is a proven 19-step process of adjustment to the loss of love and to rebuild the new you. This process can take some time

GET OUT GET FREE

to work through so be gentle with yourself. Managing your decisions going forward, after you reach your goal. Take short easy steps:

- Nobody can make you feel inferior without your permission.
- Take an inventory of who you are.
- Make a list of your positive qualities.
- Make a victory list of your past successes.
- Read other people's stories.
- Listen to motivational people who build up mankind for a positive uplift.
- Do something for someone else that you expect nothing in return for.
- Be a quitter – quit smoking, over-eating, stressing, over-loving.
- Choose your friends and associates who will support you.
- Learn to read.
- Get in shape.
- Make yourself up, dress up and go out.
- Use a role model to visualise the person you're becoming.
- Be conscious of what you're allowing into your world.
- Do a course to grow your confidence and knowledge.
- Join the smiling and confident club.

STOPPING THE CYCLE OF VIOLENCE

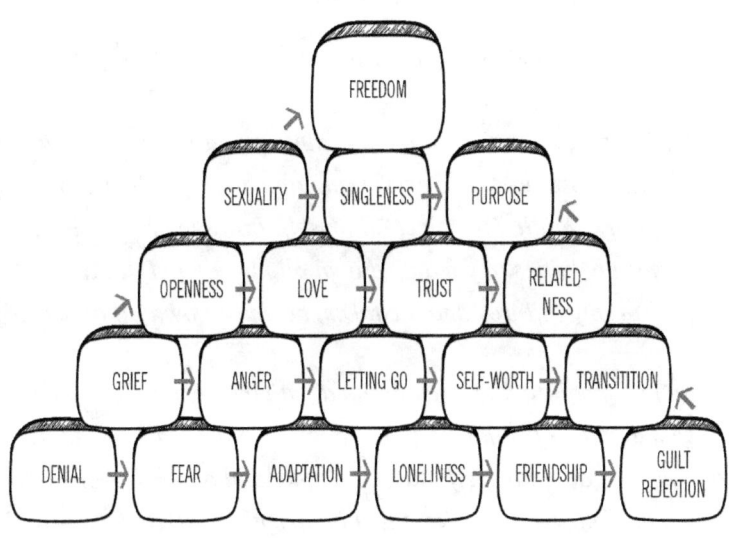

My declaration of Self Esteem *by Virginia Satir:*

I AM ME

In all the world there is no one else exactly like me...

Everything that comes out of me is authentically mine, because I alone chose it - I own everything about me, my body, my feelings, my mouth, my voice, all myself, I own my fantastic, my dreams, my hopes, my fears - I own all my triumphs and successes, all my failures and mistakes, because I own all of me...

I can become intimately acquainted with me, by doing so I can love me and be friendly with me in all my parts - I know there are aspects about myself that puzzle me, and other aspects that I do not know - but as long as I am friendly and loving with myself, I can courageously and hopefully look for the solutions to the puzzles, and for ways to find out more about me...

However, I look and sound, whatever I say and do, and whatever I think and feel at a given moment in time is authentically me - if later some parts of how I looked, sounded, thought and felt, turn out to be unfitting, I can discard that which is unfitting, keep the rest and invent something new for that which I discarded - I can see, hear, feel, think and say and do. I have the tools to survive, to be close to others, to be productive and to make sense and order out of the world of people and things outside myself - I own me, and there I can engineer me...

I am me and I AM OKAY.

Your legal rights

"It's gamesmanship. Sometimes it is not fair but if it follows the law, it's admissible in court" - Michelle Renee (PSTD & Violence against women and children).

FDV is becoming more acknowledged. Each State Government has their own policing and civil legal system, which is separate to the Commonwealth Government's family law system which is federal.

As each State Government is different in naming conventions, I mention *Local Court* which I am referring to a State Government's Local Court in your town or city which can also be called Magistrates Court in some states. An Applicant or Plaintiff means the person making the application. The Defendant or Respondent is the person responding to an application made in the Court.

The *Family Law Act 1975* is the major piece of legislation that governs the operation of family law in Australia. The main Courts exercising jurisdiction under the *Family Law Act* are the *Family Court of Australia* and the *Federal Circuit Court* which is vested with concurrent jurisdiction in matters involving less risk and complexity.

However, in Western Australia they have their own family court, the *Family Court of Western Australia* which exercises both State and Commonwealth jurisdiction. The main piece of legislation governing family law in Western Australia is the *Family Court Act 1997*, that covers de-facto couples, with the *Family Law Act 1975* applying to married couples that have divorce, children and property related issues.

When I refer to the Family Court, I mean either the *Family Court of Australia*, the *Family Court of Western Australia* or the *Federal Circuit Court*. The appropriate Court you make your application in will depend on your location and the legal issues in your matter.

Comprehending what each legal system provides will give you knowledge to protect you and your children against ongoing abuse and the abuser's power to use the legal systems against you. The *Family Court Act* overrides the restraining orders made within the Local Courts of each state, though you can request that the Family Court make parenting orders that maintain regular contact methods with children and address any risk factors in order to prevent further abuse from occurring.

Often an abuser has more financial power than their victim. Victims can become homeless, jobless, childless and lack the support of their prior community, friends or family due to FDV. Given that victims are in a powerless position, abusers continue to assert their power and control to make the victim retreat into a subservient position.

Having an understanding of your legal rights is paramount. You need the knowledge and power to assert the boundaries required, regardless of whether you are in a position to pay for legal representation, have access to the Government's *Legal Aid* service, or have to self-represent in court.

This chapter will give you a general overall outlay on how the systems work, explain how you ask for your rights and how to assert your continued boundaries toward your abuser.

If you approach the legal system the right way, you can get results. You must clearly understand how the process works so that you can achieve the boundaries you wish to set with your abuser, as well as know how to ask, protect your rights or instruct your legal representation to reduce costs and lengthy processes.

Keep in mind, these legal systems can and do fail occasionally, and it is imperative that you know your rights, so that you can re-approach the system if necessary, by way of appeal.

As abusers can attempt to further control or abuse you through the legal systems, it is important that you know your rights, particularly when you cannot afford or cannot obtain legal representation.

Self-representation may be a terrifying process for you, when you don't understand your legal rights and the processes within each court system. Self-representation is easy but daunting at the same time, though the courts are more lenient for people who self-represent, especially the Family Court.

Understanding how the process works is your first barrier and

I hope to cover the basics in this chapter. Most Court websites have access to resources, information and the forms required, although courts will not give you legal advice, they can guide you with completing forms and the processes required. If you choose or have to self-represent, there are also community legal services and programs that specialise in FDV support and legal assistance.

Restraining orders are named differently in Australian States:

- Australian Capital Territory: Domestic Violence Protection Order (governed by the *Domestic Violence and Protection Orders Act 2008*)

- New South Wales: Apprehended Domestic Violence Order (governed by the *Crimes (Domestic and Personal Violence) Act 2007*)

- Northern Territory: Domestic Violence Protection Order (governed by the *Domestic and Family Violence Act 2007*)

- Queensland: Domestic Violence Protection Order (governed by the *Domestic and Family Violence Protection Act 2012*)

- South Australia: Intervention Order (governed by the *Intervention Orders (Prevention of Abuse) Act 2009*)

- Tasmania: Family Violence Orders or Police Family Violence Orders (governed by the *Family Violence Act 2004*)

- Victoria: Family Violence Intervention Order (governed by the *Family Violence Protection Act 2008*)

- Western Australia: Family Violence Restraining Order (governed by the *Restraining Orders Act 1997*)

YOUR LEGAL RIGHTS

You can make an application at your Local Court or you can approach the police to make the application on your behalf for the restraining order. In some states where you may have to self-represent, there are community legal services which can assist you with an application for a restraining order.

Since 25 November 2017 every restraining order related to domestic violence is nationally recognised and enforceable under the National Domestic Violence Order scheme. If you have a restraining order made prior to this date, you can and should apply to the Court to have your order nationally recognized. This means that if you obtain a restraining order in one state, it is also enforceable in another.

Making an application and obtaining a restraining order does not result in the other party (the abuser) having a criminal record. However, breaching a restraining order is a criminal offence which may result in them having a criminal record. The penalty for a breach of a restraining order may result in fines and/or imprisonment. Indeed, several breaches of a restraining order will often result in imprisonment. Do not respond to a breach of the order by the other party, instead report it to the Police immediately, as in the event that the person bound by the order is charged for the breach. If you respond to a breach may cause the Court to vary or cancel the order.

After a restraining order is made by the Court, you can still apply to the Court to have it varied or cancelled if for example, it is causing you hardship or there has been a change in circumstances.

Should I get a restraining order?

When you get out of a FDV relationship the violence will more than likely increase, and this is the time when you are at your most vulnerable. You need protection, as abusers have a dire need to maintain power and control over you.

Victims in fear of their lives are in that position because of the violence they have been exposed to. However, some abusers do in fact follow through with their threats, including death threats, threats to kill themselves or your children. If you are in fear of your life or you believe your children are at risk, you need to seek immediate help!

People say, *"restraining orders are not worth the paper they are printed on."* However, for most abusers they are the first boundary that you set. For others it can escalate the abuse into a victim's murder. Do not be one of the statistics. If you think your abuser is capable of murder or if they have made threats of that nature, you need to have a safety plan and plan your escape secretly, carefully and purposefully. You may need extra assistance from professionals who are trained in the field of FDV.

I recommend that every victim of FDV obtain a restraining order as soon as required, and prior to making an application to Family Court. The timing is imperative for your protection as well as for gaining the assistance you need.

Although you may have fears in leaving your abuser, getting a restraining order can give you the extra protection and credibility you need. When attempting to set boundaries through the legal system, a restraining order provides evidence that FDV has occurred, and this is especially important when ongoing contact is

YOUR LEGAL RIGHTS

required because there are children involved. Your abuser may continue to attempt to assert power, control and abuse towards you and/or the children, as you continue to co-parent after separation.

If you fail to get a restraining order prior to making an application to the Family Court for parenting orders, this could work against you. The restraining order shall make it clear to the Family Court that they need to protect you and the children from witnessing or being at risk of being exposed to any further family violence.

The definition of family violence is very wide and can capture behavior that is not just physical abuse but includes financial, emotional and psychological abuse and a restraining order has conditions that stop the person bound from doing things they would normally be able to continue to do. Though this list is not exhaustive, here is a list of things you may wish to consider preventing the abuser from doing in your restraining order:

- Contacting or communicating with you in any way, including by text, phone calls, emails, or asking other people to do so, which usually come with exceptions of other than through a legal representative or to attend mediation;
- Coming near where you live, work or other premises you may frequent;
- Publishing on social media any material about you;
- Monitoring, hacking or using other technology or surveillance devices to track your movement or communications;
- Engaging in any other like behavior that stalks, intimidates or harasses you;

- Damaging or destroying property;
- The manner in which you, the protected person, or the person bound shall have property returned to them and/or access to a former home;
- That the person bound must not be in possession of any firearms or obtain a firearms license;
- Cause or encourage another person to do anything prohibited by the order.

Matters the Local Court will take into account when deciding on your application for a restraining order, may include the following:

- The need to ensure that the person seeking protection is protected from family violence;
- The need to prevent behavior that could reasonably be expected to cause the person seeking protection that they will have family violence committed against them;
- The need to ensure the wellbeing of children by protecting them from family violence, behavior referred to in the paragraph above or otherwise being subjected or exposed to family violence;
- The accommodation needs of the respondent and the person seeking protection;
- The past history of the respondent and the person seeking protection with respect to applications under this Act, whether in relation to the same act or persons as are before the court or not;

YOUR LEGAL RIGHTS

- Hardship that may be caused to the respondent if the order is made;
- Any existing family orders;
- Other current legal proceedings involving the respondent or the person seeking to be protected;
- Any criminal convictions of the respondent;
- Any police orders made against the respondent;
- Any previous similar behavior of the respondent whether in relation to the person seeking to be protected or otherwise;
- Any police incident reports relating to the respondent;
- Any risk assessment, or risk-relevant information, relating to the relationship between the respondent and the person seeking to be protected;
- Any other matters the court considers relevant.

The Court needs to be satisfied that family violence has occurred and that there are reasonable grounds to believe that if the order is not made the Respondent will commit further acts of family violence against the person seeking protection.

Restraining orders are initially made on an interim basis to give the other party a chance to respond, before they become final orders. Their duration will depend on the circumstances, though the default position is usually 2 years. Where the matter is urgent, the police are empowered to make temporary violence restraining orders to protect you and the children from family violence.

Sometimes Family Court cases can go on for years, and if your restraining order has expired, or if there are other circumstances that occur, then you may need to apply for an extension. In the event that you need to apply for the extension of your restraining order, and have current matters before the Family Court, the abuser may claim that you are seeking to use this against them in Family Court, which could cause the Court to question the extension of the restraining order.

Parental Alienation

Parental Alienation is child abuse and is a serious child protection matter. Parental Alienation is where one parent attempts to turn the children against the other and/or other family members, painting a negative picture using manipulation, psychological coercion and isolation or occurs when a parent is abusive.

There are two forms of parental alienation:

- **Realistic estrangement**, in which a parent's abusive behaviours, including substance abuse, result in the child not wanting to see an abusive parent.

- **Pathological estrangement**, which relates to a child's family relationships and which is not a rational response to the behaviour of the other parent. It results in the child being brainwashed against the other parent and/or family members.

Primarily, pathological estrangement occurs when a parent wishes to exclude the other parent from the life of the child. This can be in ways of punishment, disrespect, put-downs, blame, false accusations, hostility, unwarranted fear, exposure to court proceedings, or protecting the child from the 'evil' other, to accomplish their agenda without regard to the needs of the children. Loyalty and favoritism toward themselves are used, alienating

YOUR LEGAL RIGHTS

the other parent. It often leads to long-term or even permanent estrangement of a child and is regarded as a form of psychological abuse that increases the risk of mental and physical illness in a child.

Abusers often cause their own realistic estrangement as they continue to cause fears and damage their relationship with the child, their protective parent and others. The abusers do not want to lose control, want power, be exposed, accountable or responsible for their actions and can use parental alienation against you whilst you are attempting to protect the child and it is extremely important to ensure you understand this when making applications to the Family Court.

The constant bickering between the parties can be seen to be two adults who cannot communicate or co-parent, which can fall into the category of either your willingness and ability to facilitate and encourage a meaningful relationship between the child and other parent, or your attitude to the child and your responsibilities of parenthood you demonstrate. Both things are considerations that the Family Court will take into account when determining the best interests of the child and any parenting orders it makes. If the Family Court believes on the evidence before it that one parent is alienating the other parent, the Family Court may make an order that is unfavorable to them.

For realistic estrangement without a restraining order and:

- **you have an existing application for orders in the Family Court**, the abuser may respond that you are controlling and preventing them from having access to their child by either responding with an application seeking the child live with them and for sole parental responsibility as orders sought.

They may claim your behaviours are isolating them from their child, regardless of whether you are or not, which can work against you in Family Court. The Family Court can be very harsh on parents who do not have the best interests of the children at heart or who harm them in any way, so painting you as the parent causing them to be alienated often results in the abuser receiving more access or even full care and responsibility of the child. This is why a restraining order is important to show that you have encountered FDV and are protecting both yourself and the children when making the application in the Family Court. If you fit into these circumstances, ensure that you put in writing to the abuser the issue and supporting doctor's recommendations for a psychological assistance or assessment, though be mindful that the abuser likes to twist things and may use it to further substantiate their claims of being alienated and the psychological assessor being biased.

- **no application with the Family Court**, then ensure that there are methods of contact re the children if appropriate and safe, even if only through a legal representative or other independent person such as a family member. This may avoid the abuser claims of isolation or issues when making decisions without their written agreement, including to inform the other parent of any recommendations from the child's health care professionals.

For realistic estrangement with a restraining order and

- **the children are not protected by the order**, the abuser may be restricted by that order for contacting you to have access to the children unless through legal representation or by mediation, it is sometimes wise, as a legal tactic that you wait to see whether the abuser will make an application for parenting orders on the Family Court. However, if you have grave fears for the children's or your safety, receive threats of taking the children away or not return them, make the application to the Family Court immediately.

- **the children are protected by the order**, the abuser will be restricted by that order from contacting you or your children. In this case, you may wish to wait for the abuser to make an application for parenting orders on the Family Court or to have or possibly have any existing orders amended.

- **parenting orders exist**, then make an application to the Family Court for varied parenting order, which may be appropriate to include with it the form *"Notice of Child Abuse, Family Violence or Risk of Family Violence."*

For pathological estrangement you need to protect your child from harmful parenting and may need to take the necessary steps for obtaining psychological assessments and support, in order to substantiate your claims and have it addressed in your parenting orders. You can request the Family Court to make an order for the recommendations to assist for a psychological assessment.

Attending Local Court

Depending on your state of Australia, you may need to attend Court to make an application for a restraining order yourself, or you can engage legal representation to do so. Alternatively you can approach the Police who may be able to make the application for a restraining order on your behalf. Once the order is made the police will then serve the order on the Respondent, which will initially be made on an interim basis and advise them of the next court date. At the initial hearing for your restraining order application, the respondent may agree to or object to the application, or possibly not appear at all. If the Respondent doesn't attend the application may be made in their absence. If agreed to by the Respondent, the restraining order can be made by consent. If the Respondent wishes to object to the order, if no further listings are required the Magistrate will set the matter down for a trial. When the Court hears the matter, you will need to provide further evidence as to why you should have the order made by the Court. In the meanwhile, on the side of caution the Court will generally issue an interim restraining order. If the court does not make an order, you can appeal within a set time period.

If you need an interpreter, ensure you advise the Court before your Court date.

Sometimes, though not often, the abuser may not have been served the restraining order and the Court may need to adjourn the matter.

Occasionally, a Respondent may request that the matter be transferred to another Court location. Be aware that this may be a tactic to prevent you from asking the court to change a *Family Court parenting order* under *68R* of the *Family Court Act*.

Evidence for Local Court

If your abuser has refused to accept the restraining order the matter will be listed for a trial and you will need evidence, of circumstances where your abuser is denying the abuse.

Physical abuse is easier to prove using police reports and records, photos, witnesses and medical reports. Psychological abuse is much more damaging and more difficult, but it is still possible to prove. As explained in previous chapters, seeking a psychologist willing to have their records of your appointments and report/s subpoenaed to Court is necessary, in addition to keeping for example diarised records, any text and email messages and asking anyone else who has witnessed the behavior whom you may be able to be called upon as a witness.

Unfortunately, in some states of Australia, the law prevents you from using recorded evidence in Court without the respondent's permission. Therefore, obtaining their permission when recording them by using words like *"you are being recorded"* in the recording obtains their permission, as they have been advised that you are recording them. Then the recording can be used as admissible evidence in a Court. In the Family Court the evidence can be admissible if it's probative and relevant and the admission of the evidence is desirable, at the discretion of the Court. Check the laws in your state as it is also a criminal offence in some states to record someone without their consent.

Evidence for Family Court

Proving FDV isn't as simple as having a restraining order, especially if it is only an interim restraining order, though the Court will usually err on the side of caution. As explained earlier, if you do not obtain this prior to your application to Family Court, it is sometimes more difficult to obtain a restraining order when you have current matters in the Family Court and your abuser is claiming that it is a reason as to why you are seeking the order, is to use it against them in the Family Court. The Local Court does not like to work against the jurisdiction of the Family Courts, particularly so far as it concerns children.

Generally, the usual rules of evidence governed by the relevant Evidence Acts do not apply in child related proceedings, at the discretion of the Family Court, though the Court can give such weight to the evidence (if any) as it sees fit as a consequence. It will assist you with your matter when FDV is present to make your application to the Family Court with the restraining order, and complete the form *"Notice of Child Abuse, Family Violence or Risk of Family Violence"* with the application. This will also notify and trigger the child protection authorities to report on the matters, though the authorities will also look at you as you are in the system now, so be aware. In fact, your life will now also be under the microscope, so if there are any issues it is important that you are aware and are proactively taking steps to address any risk factors yourself. It is not uncommon for victims of family violence to lose their children for mental health and family violence reasons. It is best to cooperate with authorities and address any risks as this now alerts them to you, your abuser, your children and your family unit.

If abusers abuse you, they will often be abusing your children during visitation. Ensure you have diarised discussions with your abuser and events, or your children's reported events, detailing any instances where this occurs. These events are best in hand writing with an ink pen, dated and detailed with the events, preferably in a diary or by raising concerns by a conversation in writing for example by text message or in email correspondence. For example, if your child returns late, unfed or unkept, then you di-

YOUR LEGAL RIGHTS

arise when, where and how your child is being neglected. If you are abused verbally upon changeover, diarise this. Take photos your child and recordings without their knowledge, when they return from visitation. Make sure reports are made to your health professionals without delay and any reports made to your State's Child Protection Department by anyone who witnessed the child abuse, if necessary.

Family Court Mediation

Prior to filing an application in the Family Court, you need to attend mediation and it may be useful as it may help you resolve any issues. The initial advice given to anyone is not to go to Family Court, which is expensive, confronting, exhausting and stressful! In order to file your application in the Family Court you need either a mediation certificate or you need to apply for an exemption.

With FDV present, or perhaps if the matter may be urgent as the case may be, you can apply for an exemption from mediation and file that with your parenting order application.

Mediation is often used by abusers as another way of attempting to assert power and control over you. They may not agree to anything and claim that you are insane or making false statements to alienate their children from them. In the event that your abuser refuses to participate in or participates but not in any meaningful way, you will still be provided a mediation certificate

Mediators are skilled in helping you both come to agreement on parenting agreement which can be executed in the form of *Consent Orders* or a *Parenting Plan*, so that you do not need to proceed through the court system. The important thing to note with a parenting plan is that unlike consent orders, any agreement made in the form of a Parenting Plan is not enforceable by the Court, though will be taken into account in the event that you do later need to initiate proceedings in the Family Court.

The issue with abusers is that they often use mediation as an opportunity to continue to abuse you. You can advise your mediator that you do not wish to be in the same room and need staggered times, arriving after your abuser or leaving beforehand, ensuring you are safe for the mediation appointment. FDV is a common experience and mediators will often advise of possible outcomes. I have often heard many stories of victims being misled by mediators, as they have limited time, limited knowledge of your situation, nor are they trained legal professionals. You have rights with your mediator, if you are not happy or feel they are biased, contact the management or request a change in mediator. Lawyers do undertake mediation and have accreditation to do so, this option is more expensive but a good investment if you think your issues may be able to be resolved with mediation.

Legal Representation

When you engage legal representation, such as Legal Aid or a Solicitor/Lawyer who specialises in Family Law, you should fully understand the process. You engage them, not the other way around. Yes, you pay them, and they may have knowledge that you don't about court processes, but you are completely entitled to know exactly what they are doing and why they are doing it. Solicitors and Lawyers are in business to make money. Unfortunately, it can be common for some to increase the aggravation between the parties which causes the matter to drag out longer, increasing their ongoing income. Ensure that your instructions to your lawyer are clear about exactly what you want and avoid long telephone conversations and sending lengthy emails. This will help reduce your costs and feather their financial nest.

You must be very clear that you are experiencing FDV and about inform your lawyer about any significant risks associated with your matter. If you have an issue, even if it reflects negatively upon you it is important that you advise your lawyer so they are ready for it and can properly advise you of the best way forward. Don't ever lie to your lawyer! Because, if it comes out later this will catch your lawyer off guard and will not be helpful to you or your case. Ensure that all the information provided in your affidavit is true and correct to assist your lawyer to help you by substantiating the abuse with evidence, for example being proactive in seeking the relevant support or specialist reports that will assist you, your children and the Family Court.

Understand that Legal Aid usually does not represent you for property matters in the Family Court. You must proceed with self-representation or paid legal representation for this type of application.

Be aware that Legal Aid may only fund certain stages of your Family Court matter and may result in having little or no support beyond that stage. Sadly, some legal representatives focus on their higher paying clients which results in some Legal Aid clients being left behind in support and legal representation due to the low payment rates they obtain doing Legal Aid work.

When an abuser continues their abuse through legal means, it is imperative that you instruct your legal representation of what you want. You can instruct any legal representative to request more time, psychological reviews, special orders for schooling or health issues.

Your application for parenting orders

First impressions count, perception is a powerful thing, especially in the Family Court when you are standing before a Judge, Magistrate or Registrar. People judge you based how well presented you are as to the type of person you are, although not fair, it does happen. Women should dress appropriately with short or long sleeve shirt, a cardigan or blazer and no strappy singlet tops unless covered by the outer garment together with a skirt or tailored pants. Men should be in a collared shirt, preferably in a suit or blazer with tailored pants. Avoid casual clothes, joggers and t-shirt fabrics if possible.

The Family Court isn't concerned about two bickering parents, or their emotional or financial circumstances when it comes to deciding on the 'best interests of the child.' Parents don't have rights, it's the children who have rights and there is no such thing as "custody" under the current law. Your emotional rollercoaster is something you need to manage and your finances are your responsibility.

I recall my own and many others' experiences of Family Court, when I say it can be uncaring of the emotional torment that the entire process places upon us. To say Family Court is an emotional rollercoaster cannot begin to describe the highs and lows of the many months and years of unknown outcomes. The outcomes will depend upon the image you portray of who you are, possibly the respondent's ability to obscure their parenting abilities with

YOUR LEGAL RIGHTS

lies, deceit and financial capabilities, and the Judge or Magistrate's mood and perception of what is really going on. Asking a court system to make life altering decisions for the wellbeing of you and your children is terrifying to say the least, but someone has to intervene on your behalf and attempt to set boundaries with your abuser.

From the Court's perspective, an application for parenting orders can only be decided based upon the paperwork that is filed before the Court. Affidavits are statements of your facts about what has occurred or is occurring.

Shared Care is different to *Equal Parental Responsibility* as defined by the Family Court Act. Shared Care means each parent has 50% care of the child. Depending on numerous things such as the child's age and any practical difficulties, the Family Court may not agree that shared parenting is appropriate and, in the child's best interest. Who the children live with and what contact they have with the other parent is determined in accordance with what is in their best interest. As already mentioned, one thing that abusers often do is seek a change of residence for the children to live with them, regardless as to whether it is in the child's best interest or not. It is a tactic designed to hurt and exercise power and control over you, in circumstances where they don't even want the children to, nor could they properly care for the children if the children were ordered to live with them. This is a common challenge to a parenting order application should you make one, particularly when you are dealing with an abuser.

Where there are no Court orders in place, *section 61C (1)* of the Family Law Act provides that each parent of a child under 18 years has parental responsibility for the child. *Section 61B* defines parental responsibility as all the duties, powers, responsibilities and authority, which, by law, parents have in relation to their children. *Section 61DA (1)* provides that when making a parenting order the Court must apply a presumption that it is the best interests of the child for the child's parents to have equal shared parental responsibility. However, the presumption does not apply if there are reasonable grounds to believe that a parent of the child or a person who lives with the parent of the child has engaged in abuse of the child, or another child, was a member of that parent's family, or there is FDV present.

Equal Parental Responsibility it where the parents both share decision making for the children.

Sole Parental Responsibility is where one parent makes all the decisions for the children.

Abusers can and do use the child against you and you need to be one step ahead of how they operate. What tactics do they normally use to coerce you into the position they want? Will they use the Court system to get more of what they want; control over you and the children?

It is when you cannot agree on these matters that parenting orders can be put in place to deal with the issues of; for example, contact and communication. These can also be executed in the form of consent orders, where both parties are able to reach an agreement.

The Family Court takes FDV very seriously and will usually provide further protection for the children to manage any risks and prevent them from experiencing or being exposed to family violence. The Court may make changes such as children being

YOUR LEGAL RIGHTS

dropped off and picked up in a public place or even at a Police station, children being dropped off or picked up by a family member, or the abuser being allowed supervised contact only. When FDV is involved, or you believe the children are at risk in the other parents care, it is recommended that you request the Court make orders for supervised contact through a registered service. These services monitor, report on the contact, and you have no contact with the abuser during the children's supervised contact visitation with the other parent. Once this is monitored, reported, the children feel safer, and the violence towards you has settled, then the Family Court may manage any risks, progress the matter to unsupervised contact for the other parent if all is progressing well.

The Family Court also understands there are circumstances when removing your children from their home, schooling and community is paramount to their emotional, physical and psychological wellbeing. In extreme circumstances making such decisions is acceptable and necessary to protect your children, though you should seek support and legal advice first if this is your situation.

If for example, you have children in a private school and the abuser is financially attempting to punish you after leaving the relationship and your attempts in writing to get them to agree to a school change is futile, the Family Court may see the abuser as trying to manipulate you. In another example, your child may be bed-wetting and having nightmares, and your abuser may refuse to allow the child medical or psychological help, in which case you should consult your doctor for the recommended referral and seek the help the child needs. In general the abuser may claim that you are neglecting the child if you don't seek help. You may also need to inform them of the child's treatment required and show your attempts to co-parent.

When you are considering what parenting orders you need in place you should think ahead about possible issues that may arise in the future such as education, special occasions, medical issues and emergencies, travel, and include orders that allow for flexibility, bearing in mind these will continue until the child is age of 18. The typical wording of an order that gives you flexibility with your orders are the words *"or as otherwise agreed by the parties in writing"* as changing parenting orders, or not having a particular issue dealt with in your orders can be as costly and stressful as getting them in the first place, so it is important to think ahead and cover all foreseeable aspects of a child's life.

Sample parenting orders to assist you can be found online at:

https://getoutgetfree.com/gogfdownloads.

Here's a list of different issues you may need to consider when creating a parenting order:

- **Parental responsibility**: who will have parental responsibility for the child, will it be equally shared or sole parental responsibility

- **Living arrangements**: is it a shared care arrangement, or which parent will the child live with.

- **Contact**: There are four types of contact namely, shared care, substantial and significant time, supervised and no contact at all. In the case of substantial and significant time, when will the child spend time with the other parent and between what regular days and times, and additional times such as school holidays or as otherwise agreed.

- **Changeover**: It is recommended that your parenting orders deal with changeovers, particularly if FDV is involved. Where will changeovers take place? For example, in a public place, commonly McDonalds or a Police Station is a convenient location or at the children's school during the school term by the parents at the commencement and conclusion of their care. Who will facilitate the changeover? for example is changeover to occur between the parties or a nominee on their behalf.

- **Communication**: How will the other parent communicate with the child, for example by telephone or online, at a particular time, or perhaps other significant people such as grandparents. What times is the other parent permitted to call and when can you call when the child is living with the other parent? What privacy do you want for your child when communicating with the child and how long can the phone calls continue for? Parenting orders can also deal with how the parents communicate with each other, such as by phone only in the case of an emergency and at any other times via text message or perhaps through a communication book.

- **Special occasions**: It is recommended that parenting orders deal with special occasions for example Christmas, Birthdays, Mother's Day and Father's Day, or any other special event, such as, but not limited to, a wedding, birthday or funeral of any immediate family member. These events may fall on the other parent's time with the child. This becomes an issue where the relationships are often difficult, particularly when FDV is involved, and the you may not be able to reach an agreement with the other parent.

- **Medical**: Parenting orders can deal with for example how each parent shall inform each other as to any medical emergencies or health issues concerning the child whilst in their care, including providing access to information and records and contact details of health professionals who may provide medical treatment or health services to the child.

- **Education and extra-curricular activities**: Parenting orders can deal with education issues such as what school will they attend, the payment of any school fees, who will receive school reports and how they be received, will one or both parents be at liberty to attend school events or do special arrangements need to be made. What extra-curricular activities will the children attend, who will attend and will both or one parent pay for this?

- **Contact with other people**: Who else should be considered in your parenting orders. Does the child have grandparents, aunts, uncles or other significant people where the abuser may try to interfere with the child's relationship in communicating or spending time with them? Consider any other people you may wish to avoid your children having contact with.

- **Travel and passport arrangements**: Travel and any passport issues can also be dealt with in a parenting order. If a parent wishes to travel outside the metropolitan area, state or overseas, parenting orders can restrict travel without both parties consent and manage communication, notice, response and consent issues, specify what information will be provided to the other parent, such as where they are travelling and between what days, provide for any evidence of the travel, an itinerary, methods of travel and accommodation, and.in the event this interferes with the other parent's time how any lost time will be made up, are there any passport issues? Abusers often withhold consent when you are attempting to apply for a passport for your child as a form of abuse. The Court can direct a party to do all acts necessary and sign all documents to ensure the child's passport is issued or renewed, or if required make an order for the issue of the passport without the consent of the other parent. The Court can also order the passport to be delivered up to the Court in the case of risk. If you have fears that your abuser shall take the children out of the country without returning them to punish you, you need to seek urgent legal advice. One of the options is for the child to be placed on the airport watchlist by order of the Family Court. It is important to note that it is an offence to take the child out of the Country without the consent of both parents, if you have a current parenting application matter in the Family Court or without appropriate orders of the Family Court. If you are in fear of the abuser removing the Children from the country, avoid applying for a passport to reduce your fears and concerns this occurring.

- **Injunctions**: Injunctions are orders made by the Court that require a person to do or refrain from doing a particular thing. Some common examples of injunctions made in the Family court include; preventing the denigration of both or either parent, restraining parents from discussing the Court proceedings, exposing the children or protecting a parent from family violence, which may include preventing them from going to the other parent's residence or former matrimonial home.

- **Other arrangements**; what happens if you are unexpectedly unable to care for the child, are there special arrangements that need to be made for different children if for example your child has a medical condition or other special needs, including age. Is there any particular behavior or perhaps accommodation concerns in relation to the other parent that ought to be addressed, and what happens in the event of a dispute about the arrangements/orders in place.

Breach of parenting orders

If the other parent is not complying with the parenting orders made by the Family Court, then they may be in breach. Abusers will often breach orders as a form of abuse. They will attempt to force you into submitting into their demands. To make clear boundaries for the abuser, follow the orders explicitly, as you must both comply with any orders made by the Family Court or you may also be in breach.

A contravention is considered to have occurred if a person:

1. Intentionally fails to comply with the order;
2. Made no reasonable attempt to comply with the orders;
3. Intentionally prevented compliance with the order or a person bound by it;
4. Aided or abetted a contravention of the order by a person who is bound by it; and
5. Does not have a reasonable excuse for contravening the order.

If your abuser refuses to follow the order for when a child is re-

YOUR LEGAL RIGHTS

quired to have contact with them, you do not have to make other arrangements if the orders do not provide for this. For example, if they refuse or miss changeover as stipulated in the orders and demand alternate arrangements to suit themselves, then you do not have to comply. There may will be times you will need to rearrange your schedule due to the inability of the other party to be a reliable and consistent parent. However, often abusers will mess your times around, especially if you have something organised to do alone when your children are in the care of the other parent.

Occasionally parents will not engage in changeover as they should according to a Parenting order or in other cases refuse and not return the child to you.

If the child, who normally lives with you, has not been returned to you, regardless of whether you have Parenting orders in place or not, you can apply to the Family Court for a *Recovery Order*. If a recovery order is made it will direct all state and federal Police to find and recover the child, with the power to search any place, vehicle or vessel they have reasonable cause to suspect the child is located. It is suggested that you make this application immediately without delay, so that the Court will not consider the new living arrangements that the respondent has provided for the children. Abusers often keep the children and then respond to the application that you are an unfit parent as another way of punishing or abusing you which then places you and your children in a precarious situation having to justify why the children should live with you.

If you are unaware of your child's location, and occasionally these are required in conjunction with a recovery order, the Court can make a *Location Order* which will engage the assistance of

Police and other government agencies such as Centrelink or direct certain people who may be aware to provide any information as to the whereabouts of the child.

If you wish to make a change to a Parenting order temporarily, and the orders provide for this, even if the orders don't stipulate it, ensure that you put this in writing to the abuser so that everything is documented. Diarise any breaches in the event you do not file a *Contravention Application* for a minor breach and keep records in the event that you do have to return to the Family Court for one reason or another, or later to file a *Contravention Application*. If there are any issues or practical difficulties, the Court may wish to also vary the orders or make additional orders to prevent any further breaches in the future. The Family Court wants to get things back on track for your family and children, and does not necessarily want to punish the breaching parent, it does attempt to build and manage the relationship between the parents and child as that is in the children's best interest. You can also make an application for an *Enforcement Order*, though this does not punish them for breaching the orders, unlike a contravention application.

In the event the Court finds that the order has been breached without a reasonable excuse, they can impose a penalty which may include a variation to the order, attendance at a parental education program or other community service activity, require to enter into a bond for a certain period, impose a fine or in the worst case it can result imprisonment. The party found to have contravened the order may also be ordered to pay compensation for expenses arising from the contravention to the other party and/or the other party's legal costs.

YOUR LEGAL RIGHTS

If the other parent has breached the order, write a formal document and send it to them prior to making a contravention application advising them that if they do not immediately comply with the Court orders you will make a contravention application to the Family Court. A *Breach of Parenting Order* sample letter found at https://getoutgetfree.com/gogfdownloads.

In the event that you require changes in your Parenting order and you both can agree about the changes, you can file by *Consent Parenting Orders* that can be executed as binding orders of the Court which are enforceable the same as if the Court was required to make the orders. Each case will vary; therefore, it depends as to whether you will be required to engage in the mediation process again as your mediation certificate is only valid for 12 months. The Family Court shall not take lightly the variation of change of a parenting order unless under significant change in circumstances or practical difficulty. Try your best to mediate to gain new consent orders if the current parenting orders are not working for you or the other parent.

Keep in mind the Family Court will not force a parent to spend time with a child if that parent does not want to spend time with the child.

Orders against a child's will

Unfortunately, some parents will insist that a child spend time with them against the child's wishes or without regard to their best interests, and may even seek to a change of residence, that is for the child to come and live with them. Sometimes it is a difficult balancing act between the wellbeing, the risks and the interests of child to maintain a meaningful relationship with both parents.

There are two primary considerations, that the Family Court will consider when making a parenting order in the best interests of the child:

- The need for the child to have a meaningful relationship with both parents
- The need to protect the child from any physical or psychological harm or being subjected to, or exposed to, abuse, neglect, and FDV.

There are 13 additional considerations that the Family Court will also take into account when making a parenting order in the best interests of the child:

- The child's expressed views, in the context with of child's maturity or level of understanding
- The nature of the child's relationship to the parents or other people such as relatives
- The extent to which the child's parents have taken or fail to take the opportunity in making decisions, spending time and communicating with the child
- The likely effects of any changes to the child's change in circumstances, including separation from their parents, other children or people such as grandparents
- The practical difficulty and expense of a child spending time with and communicating with a parent and whether that difficulty or expense will substantially affect the child's right to maintain personal relations and direct contact with both parents on a regular basis

YOUR LEGAL RIGHTS

- The capacity of each of the child's parents, or other person, including grandparents to provide for the needs of the child including any emotional, physical, psychological and intellectual needs

- The maturity, sex, lifestyle and background (including lifestyle, culture and traditions) of the child and of either of the child's parents, and any other characteristics of the child that the court thinks are relevant

- If the child is an Aboriginal child or a Torres Strait Islander child, the child's right to enjoy his or her Aboriginal or Torres Strait Islander culture, the likely impact any proposed parenting order would have on that right

- The attitude to the child, and to the responsibilities of parenthood, demonstrated by each of the child's parents

- Any family violence involving the child or a member of the child's family

- If a family violence order applies, or has applied, to the child or a member of the child's family

- Whether it would be preferable to make the order that would be least likely to lead to the institution of further proceedings in relation to the child;

- Any other fact or circumstance that the court thinks is relevant

Every child wants the love and protection of both parents. It is when one or both parents fail the child by neglecting their emotional, physical or psychological needs that a child may not want to have contact with a parent. If you have concerns over your child's well being, consult a university-trained professional for their advice and concerns. The Family Court can order that an *Independent Children's Lawyer (ICL)* be appointed to your matter. An ICL is a lawyer for the child and their role is to consider the needs of the child and help the Court determine what is in the best interests of the child. They may ask the Court to appoint *Single Expert Witness* which can assist the Court by providing an *Independent Report*, about the issues in your matter. This is an expensive process often costing thousands of dollars but may be beneficial to substantiate your claims in the Family Court.

What most people do not understand, is that when an abuser is threatening your child, whether it be direct or indirect threats to harm, threaten to kill or maim them or someone they love, the child can be too scared to divulge the information to a Court appointed professional such as ICL's or a single expert witness. This often places the child in further danger or exposure to an abuser. However, if you have FDV evidence such as a restraining order, the reporter generally gets a copy of the Court files. Ensure these records are provided to the ICL and any appointed Single Expert Witness so that they have sufficient information to base their opinions on, as this may prevent them from gaining full knowledge of the real facts, risks and wishes of the child.

The Family Court can make an order against the wishes of the child but will take into account those wishes and they usually carry more weight from about the age of 11-12 years old. Occasionally, the Court may make an order for a *Child Inclusive Conference* with the Courts trained *Family Consultants*, depending on the issues of the case. The Court may also order the parties to engage in a *Case Assessment Conference* before a Family Con-

YOUR LEGAL RIGHTS

sultant to assess the matter, any risks and the best interests of the child.

Ensure you do not discuss the Court proceedings with the child and allow their natural expression of their concerns and feelings about the other parent, as this may be seen as coaching the child to alienate the other parent. However, ensure that you discuss your child's fears and concerns with the ICL, consultant or expert witnesses.

Moving Forward

Personal growth is inevitable in life, you do have control over the speed in which you choose to grow. Life never stays the same, nor is everyday like 'Groundhog Day'. The weather changes, how you think and feel, and life in general changes. What you may have believed yesterday, may be challenged today. You may find more knowledge that changes how you think. You are not alone in moving forward, as it is a part of everyday life. You cannot stay stationery, even though some days may feel like you haven't moved an inch! But your awareness has!

Understanding how you entered into an abusive relationship is imperative if you are to avoid another abusive relationship. Taking responsibility for your happiness is paramount to preventing falling into the trap again, with a manipulative, control freak abuser. You may wonder how you entered into a toxic or abusive relationship, but if you knew what you do now, I bet that you wouldn't have wanted to begin that relationship! Love can convince you to stay. But when love isn't present, it convinces you

MOVING FORWARD

to leave an unhappy relationship. After all, what else are you in it for?

If fear has controlled your decisions in the past, take heart. You can overcome fear when you have knowledge and power. Once you have learnt about abusive relationships, you cannot become unaware and your choices in the future will be different if you pay attention to the warning signs and are prepared to put your safety and wellbeing above your needs for love.

Once you have your plan to escape your abusive relationship, know how to stay safe, and how to obtain the support you need, your fears will diminish significantly with the steps and knowledge that you can regain the control over your life.

There are so many resources available to assist you and you will find these resources where you can seek the support you need in your locality. In addition to those listed below, you will find more support and programs at https://getoutgetfree.com.

The types of available support services that are often free to help you are:

- The Daisy app available on Android and Apple was created by 1800RESPECT. This app provides links to support services in many languages.
- Women's refuges.
- Financial support such as Child support, Centrelink, financial counselling, charities for food, fuel, utility bills, Legal Aid, Women's Law Centres and Court Support schemes.
- Rehabilitation for perpetrators.
- Mental Health support.

- Sexual Violence support for adults and children.
- Accommodation assistance.
- Advocacy services for elder abuse, torture and trauma survivors, Migrants and CALd community.
- TAFE and University, especially with disability and FDV.
- Support for Alcohol & Drug problems.
- General counselling.
- FDV counselling.
- Crisis and emergency care.
- Disability support.
- Family support.
- State Child Protection Government agencies.
- Compensation for victims of crime for criminal injuries, bodily harm suffered, mental or nervous conditions, pregnancy resulting from an offence.
- Victim support programs.

Choosing your partners carefully

A checklist of what you want in a partner is a brilliant idea so that you can assess how your partner measures up to your needs. Barbara De Angelis's book *Are you the One for Me?* is an excellent book to read to ascertain exactly what you are looking for in a relationship and if your partner measures up to your grade. Barbara recommends that you construct a list within each of the 10 categories. Once you have that list compiled, you can then grade your prospective partner between 1 and 5 points for each item within each category's list.

She recommends how to label your wants and needs in a relationship with the following categories:

1. **Physical style**; such as height, weight, looks, grooming, body build, health, wellbeing, manners, dressing style or makeup etc.

2. **Emotional style**; such as listening skills, emotionality, romantic, kindness, loving, expression of feelings, support, commitment, loyalty, sentiment, admiration, sensitivity, trustworthiness or affection.

3. **Social style**; such as warmth, friendliness, confidence, openness, happiness, humour, socialise, sophistication, playfulness, variety, likeable, eating out/dining/movies/camping etc.

4. **Intellectual style**; such as speech, education level, ability to write/spell/read, openness to learning, absence of prejudice, having an open mind to the world and environment, seeks solutions or reads.

5. **Sexual style**; such as enjoys/wants sexual relationship, the frequency of sexual relations, sensuality, seductiveness, experience, playfulness, non-aggressiveness, touching or satisfaction.

6. **Communication style**; such as open communication, sorts problems, doesn't avoid discussions or becomes aggressive, clear and confident, enjoys talking, enjoys sharing experiences, open to criticism, jokes/humour.

7. **Professional/financial style**; such as work for success, not too tight, reliable jobs, progression in job, organised, enjoys luxury occasionally or likes finer things in life, basic necessity, wants shared/separate things, saves for future, is honest and trustworthy with finances.

8. **Personal growth style**; such as self-growth/improvement, owns faults, change and growth, understands differences, encourages growth in others, has a positive outlook or emotional maturity.

9. **Spiritual style**; such as religious beliefs, morals, ethics, treasures in life or church attendance.

10. **Interests and hobbies style**; such as television, music, reading, picnics, bush walking, camping, bike riding, animals, movies, theatre, swimming and other sports.

Once you have the total points of the categories, then you can work out your average for each category and then the total list. Barbara also recommends the 80/20 rule. If you score over 80% it might be a relationship worth investing in. If they score below 80% then you may need to put a lot of work into making the relationship a success. She also recommends that you check initially after meeting your partner, then at 3 monthly intervals as people change. If you have a healthy relationship, you can discuss the areas in which you want to improve with your partner and allow the relationship to grow.

When scoring your partner, be totally honest with yourself. Don't sell yourself short whilst doing this grading. It might sound totally strategic and it is, but it will give you the clear vision of what you are sacrificing for the love you are wanting in your life.

Do regular scoring for your new relationship. Are there areas that you cannot change with your partner and just need to accept to continue with your relationship? Make sure you are making conscious choices of what you are choosing to accept and what you are not. If you cannot change the issues with your partner that you cannot accept, then perhaps it is time to reassess the viability of the relationship. Do not give up your happiness for the sake of a relationship and continue to monitor the amount of sacrifice you offer in order to maintain the relationship.

As said once before, relationships are for relating. If you are not relating in a healthy manner, you are not relating at all. All relationships come and go, either through death or separation. Don't hold onto something where you will lose yourself. It is not worth it for you, let alone your children.

Hold your head up high. You deserve to be happy. No one can give it to you. You must claim it yourself!

References

1. Mark L. Knapp, Interpersonal Communications and Human Relationships Boston: Allyn and Bacon, 1984.
2. Robert J Sternberg, Yale University. A Triangular Theory of Love. Psychological Review,1986,Vol.93, No. 2,119-135. Found at http://pzacad.pitzer.edu/~dmoore/psych199/1986_sternberg_trianglelove.pdf
3. Robert J Sternberg, Yale University. A Triangular Theory of Love, Psychological Review,1986,Vol.93, No. 2,119-135. Found at http://pzacad.pitzer.edu/~dmoore/psych199/1986_sternberg_trianglelove.pdf
4. Australian Bureau of Statistics. (2009). National Survey of Mental Health and Wellbeing: Summary of Results, 4326.0, 2007. ABS: Canberra.
5. Ivancic, L., Perrens, B., Fildes, J., Perry, Y. and Christensen, H. (2014). Youth Mental Health Report, June 2014. Mission Australia and Black Dog Institute, Sydney.
6. Kitchener, B.A. and Jorm, A.F. (2009). Youth Mental Health First Aid: A manual for adults assisting youth. ORYGEN Research Centre, Melbourne.
7. Australian Institute of Health and Welfare. (2014). Australia's Health 2014. AIHW: Canberra.
8. Commonwealth of Australia. (2010). National Mental Health Report 2010. Canberra, Australia.
9. Australian Government, Department of Social Services, Woman's Safety: https://www.dss.gov.au/women/programs-services/reducing-violence/the-national-plan-to-reduce-violence-against-women-and-their-children-2010-2022
10. Australian Government, Department of Social Services, Woman's Safety: https://www.dss.gov.au/women/programs-services/reducing-violence/the-national-plan-to-reduce-violence-against-women-and-their-chil-

REFERENCES

dren-2010-2022

11. Australian Government, Department of Social Services, Woman's Safety: https://www.dss.gov.au/women/programs-services/reducing-violence/the-national-plan-to-reduce-violence-against-women-and-their-children-2010-2022

12. ANCROW Violence Against Women: Accurate use of key statistics, https://d2c0ikyv46o3b1.cloudfront.net/anrows.org.au/ANROWS_VAW-Accurate-Use-of-Key-Statistics.1.pdf

13. Victorian State Government, Victoria Act, Family Violence Protection Act 2008 - Sect 5, http://classic.austlii.edu.au/au/legis/vic/consol_act/fvpa2008283/s5.html

14. Chan, A. and Payne, J. (2013). Homicide in Australia 2008-09 to 2009-10, National Homicide Monitoring Program annual report, Canberra, Australia: Australian Institute of Criminology. Retrieved from: https://aic.gov.au/publications/mr/mr21

15. American Psyucicatry Association, What is Post Traumatic Stress Disorder?, https://www.psychiatry.org/patients-families/ptsd/what-is-ptsd

16. Health Direct, Nine Signs of Mental Health Issues, https://www.healthdirect.gov.au/signs-mental-health-issue

17. Australian Government, Australian Institute of Family Studies, https://aifs.gov.au/cfca/publications/long-term-effects-child-sexual-abuse

18. Australian Government, Australian Institute of Family Studies, https://aifs.gov.au/cfca/publications/long-term-effects-child-sexual-abuse-1998

19. Adorjan M, Christensen T, Kelly B, Pawluch D (2012). "Stockholm Syndrome As Vernacular Resource". The Sociological Quarterly. 53 (3): 454–74.

20. Domestic Abuse Intervention Project, 202 East Superior St, Duluth MA 55802, https://www.theduluthmodel.org/wheels/

Further information

Liz Atherton is a Life Coach & Medium who offers a range of support services for clients throughout the world.

Liz's goal in life is to help as many people as possible find true joy and understanding of the purpose and passions of their lives, and to start living them, regardless of the changes needed. She can help you become more attuned to listen to your own needs, within your relationships, including the most important relationship, with yourself.

Her first book *Mind Chatter That Matters* has helped many people around the world with learning how to listen to their Intuitive Self, moving them forward to more happiness and fulfillment.

"Happiness is found when setting boundaries within your relationships to ensure you are living according to your own values, morals and integrity. Then everything else falls into place." said Liz.

You can contact Liz at **https://lizatherton.com**, or find Liz on most social media platforms.

FURTHER INFORMATION

www.ingramcontent.com/pod-product-compliance
Lightning Source LLC
Chambersburg PA
CBHW071911290426
44110CB00013B/1349